D0741910

127720

SANTA ANA PUBLIC LIBRARY

Santa Ana, California

JOSEPH BRODSKY: SELECTED POEMS

JOSEPH BRODSKY: SELECTED POEMS

Translated from the Russian by
George L. Kline
Foreword by W. H. Auden

HARPER & ROW, Publishers
New York, Evanston, San Francisco, London

JOSEPH BRODSKY: SELECTED POEMS. English translation and Introduction copyright © 1973 by George L. Kline. Foreword copyright © 1973 by W. H. Auden. All rights reserved. Printed in the United States of America. No part of this book may be used or reproduced in any manner whatsoever without written permission except in the case of brief quotations embodied in critical articles and reviews. For information address Harper & Row, Publishers, Inc., 10 East 53rd Street, New York, N. Y. 10022. Published simultaneously in Canada by Fitzhenry & Whiteside Limited, Toronto.

FIRST U.S. EDITION

ISBN: 0-06-010484-8

LIBRARY OF CONGRESS CATALOG CARD NUMBER: 73-4065

To the memory of Wystan Hugh Auden
1907–1973

Contents

Foreword

One demands two things of a poem. Firstly, it must be a well-made verbal object that does honor to the language in which it is written. Secondly, it must say something significant about a reality common to us all, but perceived from a unique perspective. What the poet says has never been said before, but, once he has said it, his readers recognize its validity for themselves.

A really accurate judgement upon a poem as a verbal object can, of course, only be made by persons who are masters of the same mother-tongue as its maker. Knowing no Russian and therefore forced to base my judgement on English translations, I can do little more than guess. My chief reason for believing that Professor Kline's translations do justice to their originals is that they convince me that Joseph Brodsky is an excellent craftsman. For example, in his long poem *Elegy for John Donne* the word *sleep* occurs, if I have counted rightly, fifty-two times. Such repetition might very easily have become irritating and affected: in fact, it is handled with consummate art.

Again, it is clear from these translations that Mr Brodsky commands many tones of voice, from the lyric (*A Christmas Ballad*) to the elegiac (*Verses on the Death of T. S. Eliot*) to the comic-grotesque (*Two Hours in an Empty Tank*), and can handle with equal ease a wide variety of rhythms and meters, short lines, long lines, iambics, anapaestics, masculine rhymes and feminine, as in *Adieu, Mademoiselle Véronique*:

> If I end my days in the shelter of dove-wings,
> which well may be, since war's meat-grinder
> is now the prerogative of small nations,
> since, after manifold combinations,

Mars has moved closer to palms and cacti,
and I myself wouldn't hurt a housefly . . .

About the uniqueness and, at the same time, universal
relevance of a poet's vision, it is easier for a foreigner to
judge, since this does not primarily depend upon the
language in which it is written.

Mr Brodsky is not an easy poet, but even a cursory reading
will reveal that, like Van Gogh and Virginia Woolf, he has
an extraordinary capacity to envision material objects as
sacramental signs, messengers from the unseen. Here are a
few examples.

But this house cannot stand its emptiness.
The lock alone – it seems somehow ungallant –
is slow to recognize the tenant's touch
and offers brief resistance in the darkness.
('The tenant . . .')

The fire, as you can hear, is dying down.
The shadows in the corners have been shifting.
It's now too late to shake a fist at them
or yell at them to stop what they are doing.
('The fire . . .')

A hand that holds a pillow fast
is creeping down a polished bedpost,
making its way to a cloud breast
by this inept and tongue-tied gesture.
A sock, torn on a jagged rock,
twists in the dark; its curve is swan-like.
Its funnel mouth is all agog;
it stares up like a blackened fishnet.
(*Enigma for an Angel*)

Close your umbrella, as a rook would close
its wings. Its handle-tail reveals the capon.
(*Einem alten Architekten in Rom*)

It's not quite spring, but some-
thing like it.
The world is scattered now,
and crooked.
The ragged villages
are limping.
There's straightness only in
bored glances.

(*Spring Season of Muddy Roads*)

Unlike the work of some of his contemporaries, Mr
Brodsky's seems to stand outside what might be called the
Mayakovsky tradition of 'public' poetry. It never uses a
fortissimo. Indeed, original as he is, I would be inclined to
classify Mr Brodsky as a traditionalist. To begin with, he
shows a deep respect and love for the past of his native land.

The dogs, moved by old memory, still lift
their hindlegs at a once familiar spot.
The church's walls have long since been torn down,
but these dogs see the church walls in their dreams . . .

For them the church still stands; they see it plain.
And what to people is a patent fact
leaves them entirely cold. This quality
is sometimes called 'a dog's fidelity'.
And, if I were to speak in earnest of
the 'relay race of human history',
I'd swear by nothing but this relay race –
this race of all the generations who
have sniffed, and who will sniff, the ancient smells.

(*A Halt in the Desert*)

He is also a traditionalist in the sense that he is interested in
what most lyric poets in all ages have been interested in, that
is, in personal encounters with nature, human artifacts,
persons loved or revered, and in reflections upon the
human condition, death, and the meaning of existence.

His poems are a-political, perhaps defiantly so, which may explain why he has, so far, failed to win official approval, for I can find nothing in them which the sternest censor could call 'subversive' or 'immoral'. The only lines which could conceivably be called 'political' are these:

> Adieu to the prophet who said, 'Forsooth,
> you've nothing to lose but your chains.' In truth
> there's conscience as well – if it comes to that.
>
> (*A Letter in a Bottle*)

a sentiment with which, surely, any good Marxist would agree. As for his artistic credo, no poet would quarrel with

> It seems that what art strives for is to be
> precise and not to tell us lies, because
> its fundamental law undoubtedly
> asserts the independence of details.
>
> (*The Candlestick*)

After reading Professor Kline's translations, I have no hesitation in declaring that, in Russian, Joseph Brodsky must be a poet of the first order, a man of whom his country should be proud. I am most grateful to them both.

W. H. AUDEN

Introduction

Joseph Brodsky was born in Leningrad on 24 May 1940. At an early age he began to exhibit the independence of judgement which so sharply distinguishes his work. His independent cast of mind did not go unnoticed by the Soviet authorities, who repeatedly reprimanded him and, in February 1964, brought him to trial on charges of 'social parasitism', sentencing him to five years' hard labor in the Arkhangelsk region of Northern Russia. (Brodsky was in fact released after only twenty months in exile.) In June 1972 he was 'invited' to leave the Soviet Union. He spent the academic year 1972–3 as poet-in-residence and special lecturer at the University of Michigan. During the fall semester of 1973–4 he will hold a similar post at Queens College, New York.

Brodsky's independence of literary judgement appears, for example, in his characterization of Robert Frost as the greatest American poet of the twentieth century – a complex, intellectual poet, whose work, far from being comfortable and 'cracker-barrel', is a vivid revelation of the unbearable horrors of human existence. For Brodsky the tradition of Russian literature is a vital and intimate reality; but he feels closer to Derzhavin than to Pushkin, closer to Baratynsky, Annensky, and even (early) Mayakovsky than to Blok, and closer to Platonov than to Solzhenitsyn.

Brodsky's formal education came to an end in 1955, after the eighth grade. A year later his world was shaken by news of the Hungarian uprising and the 'Polish October'. He began to study Polish, and made rapid progress after 1958 when he met a girl from Warsaw who was a student at Leningrad University. She brought him books from Poland

– in both Polish and English – novels, poetry, mythology, philosophy. It was in Polish translation that Brodsky first read Faulkner and Kafka. He also read such contemporary Polish poets as Zbigniew Herbert and Czesław Miłosz, both of whom he admires enormously. He considers Miłosz, whom he is currently translating into Russian, one of the major poets of the twentieth century.

Brodsky had begun to study English in the fifth grade and continued through the eighth, but with meagre results. The language was taught in a formal and theoretical way – like Latin or Sanskrit – by incompetent teachers using inadequate texts. A decade later, during his period of exile (1964–5), he returned to the serious study of English. Equipped only with a paperback anthology of English and American poetry and an English–Russian dictionary, he spent long evenings – at the latitude of Arkhangelsk there is not much winter daylight – puzzling over the verses of Dylan Thomas, W. H. Auden, Eliot, Yeats, and Wallace Stevens. His technique was simple: he made literal translations of the first and last stanzas and then tried to 'imagine' what, poetically speaking, should come in between! More recently he has been involved in a large-scale translation of the English metaphysical poets and has translated Brendan Behan's *Quare Fellow* and Tom Stoppard's *Rosencrantz and Guildenstern are Dead*.

During his exile, but also before and after it, Brodsky vigorously pursued his project of self-education, reading such Russian poets (in addition to those already mentioned) as Osip Mandelstam and Marina Tsvetayeva, whom he considers – along with Anna Akhmatova – the greatest of the twentieth-century Russian poets. He has also read widely and deeply in Greek mythology, the Bible, and such Russian religious thinkers as Chaadayev, Dostoyevsky, Solovyov, Berdyaev, and Shestov. The last-named is one of Brodsky's favorites.

Brodsky was blessed by the friendship of Anna Akhmatova during the last five years of her life (she died early in 1966). He found her an inspiration, not only as a poet *par excellence*, but also as a perceptive and original critic, and a human being of extraordinary warmth, intelligence, profundity, and wit. She singled him out as the most gifted lyric poet of his generation and, in December 1963, described his verses as 'magical'. At that early date Brodsky had written only a handful of major poems, in particular the *Elegy for John Donne* and *Isaac and Abraham* (both 1963). Akhmatova lived to see such important works as *New Stanzas to Augusta* and *Einem alten Architekten in Rom* (both 1964), *Verses on the Death of T. S. Eliot, Two Hours in an Empty Tank*, and *A Letter in a Bottle* (all 1965). She especially admired the Eliot poem.

Brodsky's is a private, not a public, muse. His poetry is intensely personal, meditative, 'suffering'. To a certain extent he continues the elaborate and inventive poetic 'conceits' of the English Metaphysical poets, perhaps most explicitly in the untranslated *Song without Music* (1969). Brodsky is deeply concerned with the realities, beyond appearance, of love and death; communion, separation, and solitude; suffering and betrayal; sin and salvation. He also shares Shestov's 'existential' sense of the unbearable and unrationalizable horrors of human existence. One of his earliest poems has as its refrain the phrase 'in anguish unaccountable' (*A Christmas Ballad*, 1962). Gorbunov, in the long poem *Gorbunov and Gorchakov* (1965–8), declares that 'the points/ of all life's pains are focused in my breast/ as in a prism'. Later in the same poem we confront 'men, and creatures driven mad/ by ghastly lives within the womb and after/ the grave'.

One of the deepest horrors, for Brodsky, is the finality of human separation. Of divided lovers he writes:

Our farewell's the more final
since we both are aware
that we'll not meet in Heaven
or be neighbors in Hell.

(*Stanzas*, 1968)

The separation of father and son is poignantly expressed in
Odysseus to Telemachus (1972):

... Telemachus, dear boy!
To a wanderer the faces of all islands
resemble one another ...
I can't remember how the war came out;
even how old you are – I can't remember.

Grow up, then, my Telemachus, grow strong.
Only the gods know if we'll see each other
again.

Brodsky sees literature in general, and poetry in parti-
cular, as a 'mode of endurance' – a way of facing, and
perhaps surviving, the ghastliness of both public and private
life. His poetry of the mid-1960s – especially *Two Hours in
an Empty Tank* and From *The School Anthology: Albert
Frolov* (1969) – exhibits strong elements of the comic-
grotesque. His most recent poems – especially *Gorbunov and
Gorchakov, Post Aetatem Nostram* (1970), and *Nature Morte*
(1971) – show clear traces of the 'literature of the absurd'
and 'post-absurd'. Parts of *Gorbunov and Gorchakov* are
strongly reminiscent of Beckett.

Gorbunov envisages a kind of death-in-life:

'I think that a man's soul, while it still lives,
takes on the features of mortality.'

(*Gorbunov and Gorchakov*, Canto II)

Even Christ appears as a divine-human still-life, a *nature
morte*:

Mary now speaks to Christ:
'Are you my son? – or God?
You are nailed to the cross.
Where lies my homeward road?

How can I close my eyes,
uncertain and afraid?
Are you dead? – or alive?
Are you my son? – or God?'

Christ speaks to her in turn:
'Whether dead or alive,
woman, it's all the same –
son or God, I am thine.'

(*Nature Morte*, Pt X)

The Brodskyan concern with death, solitude, and salvation – and with the binding up and healing of what in human life is broken and torn – is exhibited in the *Elegy for John Donne*. This somber and powerful poem is built around two related ideas: that each item of the poet's world dies ('falls asleep') with his death, but that the world which his poetry has created is deathless. John Donne's body, at the end of the poem, is a torn and ragged coat. The conventional image of the body as a garment for the soul takes on special urgency in Donne, who refers to death as stringing heaven and earth together, like beads, on the thread of a human soul. Brodsky combines these conceits with the 'Northern' image of falling snow to form the strikingly original image of snowflake-needles stitching body to soul and earth to heaven.

... the busy snow whirls through the dark,
not melting, as it stitches up this hurt –
its needles flying back and forth. ...

For though our life may be a thing to share,
who is there in this world to share our death?

Man's garment gapes with holes. It can be torn,
by him who will, at this edge or at that.
It falls to shreds and is made whole again.
... And only the far sky,
in darkness, brings the healing needle home.

The Pasternakian 'unity of poetry and life' which is implicit in the *Elegy for John Donne* becomes explicit in *Verses on the Death of T. S. Eliot*, a poem which borrows its form and meter from Auden's *In Memory of W. B. Yeats*. A great poet has died and, as in the Donne poem, a part of the world dies with him, for 'each grave is the limit of the earth'. We who survive are left on a 'dry land of days' in which the poet's exuberant creative vitality appears as a 'January gulf'. The poet has been taken from us not by God but only by nature:

It was not God, but only time, mere time
that called him....

God would have 'called' the poet only if his creative work had been completed. But that was not Eliot's case; his time had simply run out.

The poet's immortality is secured not by civilization but by nature. Addressing Eliot directly, Brodsky declares:

Wood and field will not forget.
All that lives will know you yet.

And he adds:

If you're not recalled by stone,
puff ball drift will make you known.

The opposition of poetry, religion, and life to dead things, especially machines, is one of the central themes of *A Halt in the Desert* (1966). A Greek Orthodox church in Leningrad has been razed to make room for a glass-and-steel concert hall; this in fact happened, near Brodsky's home, during the mid-1960s. The church is alive and the neighborhood dogs, at least, are faithful to its memory; for them 'the church still stands'. But the machines that batter down the church's walls are wholly insensitive to the miracle of its life:

> ... the power shovel may have thought
> the wall a dead and soulless thing and thus,
> to a degree, like its own self. And in
> the universe of dead and soulless things
> resistance is regarded as bad form.

The other central theme in this poem concerns the relationship of Christianity to culture – an echo of Mandelstam. This is expressed in part through a play on two senses of the term 'Greek': 'Greek Orthodox' and 'Hellenic'. It seems likely that Brodsky is the only Russian poet of his generation for whom this is a live and tormenting issue.

Another of Brodsky's religious themes, that of the 'Passion' – the nature and function of religious suffering, or the religious nature and function of human suffering – is explored most fully in two long and important poems, *Adieu, Mademoiselle Véronique* (1967) and *Gorbunov and Gorchakov*. There was a Mlle Véronique in Brodsky's life, but *Adieu, Mademoiselle Véronique* is not a love poem. Rather it is a Christian meditation on the Passion theme, and an examination of the relation of erotic love to redemptive, sacrificial love. At the heart of the poem stands the Dostoyevskyan assertion that

> The total of all of today's embraces
> gives far less of love than the outstretched arms of
> Christ on the cross.

Brodsky attributes this insight to Boris Pasternak, identified in the poem only as a 'lame poet'. Pasternak in fact walked with a slight limp but tried to conceal it and was not

19

generally known to be lame. The specific reference is to the second of the *Mary Magdalene* poems in the *Dr Zhivago* cycle. Mary Magdalene, speaking directly to Christ, declares:

> Your arms stretched to the ends of the cross
> Spread wide in a vast embrace.

Gorbunov and Gorchakov, which consists of fourteen cantos each having one hundred lines, is an extended meditation in dialogue form on the themes of suffering and solitude, love and separation, betrayal and salvation. The name 'Gorbunov' suggests the Russian word for 'hunchback' (*gorbun*); Gorbunov is indeed a kind of spiritual cripple, beaten down and tormented by the world. The name 'Gorchakov' suggests the Russian word for 'bitterness' (*gorech*); Gorchakov is both a bitter man and one who embitters the lives of others, especially Gorbunov. The two men are long-term patients in a mental hospital. They share a room and talk endlessly. Having told each other everything about their former lives, they begin to tell each other about their dreams. In the end Gorchakov reports the unorthodox content of Gorbunov's dreams to the psychiatrists, who reward him by a promise of release 'at Easter time'. In the end Gorbunov emerges as a kind of Christ figure and Gorchakov as a kind of Judas figure.

In one of his most recent poems, *Nunc dimittis* (1972), Brodsky offers an account, in beautifully simple, 'Biblical' language, of the death of the holy man Simeon. Simeon serves as a bridge between the Old and the New Testament; his death is the first 'Christian death' in history. He dies – as had been foretold – as soon as he has seen the Christ child:

> The roaring of time ebbed away in his ears.
> And Simeon's soul held the form of the Child –

its feathery crown now enveloped in glory –
aloft, like a torch, pressing back the black shadows,

to light up the path that leads into death's realm,
where never before until this point in time
had any man managed to lighten his pathway.
The old man's torch glowed and the pathway grew wider.

Like Mandelstam and Tsvetayeva, Brodsky makes skill-
ful and extensive use of Greek mythology. His poetry is
filled with references to Hector, Andromache, Ajax,
Orpheus, Artemis, Athena, Aeneas, Dido, Oedipus, Odys-
seus, Telemachus, Palamedes. The poem *To Lycomedes on
Scyros* (1967) combines mythological and religious language
to drive home an intensely moral point about the duty to
resist evil:

> I quit this city, as once Theseus quit
> the labyrinth, leaving the Minotaur
> to rot, and Ariadne to make love
> with Bacchus. . . .
> When all is said and done, a murder is
> a murder. And we mortals have a duty
> to take up arms against all monsters. . . .
>
>   Men can
> return to where they have done evil deeds,
> but men do not return to where they've been
> abased. On this point God's design and our
> own feeling of abasement coincide
> so absolutely that we quit: the night,
> the rotting beast, the exultant mob, our homes,
> our hearthfires, Bacchus in a vacant lot
> embracing Ariadne in the dark.

For Brodsky, as for Rilke and Eliot, poetic language may
be said to have the same degree of 'reality' as the world;
words regularly interact with things.

In *Isaac and Abraham* the transformation, in Isaac's dream, of the word *kust* ('bush') into the word *krest* ('cross'), which takes place painfully, letter by letter, symbolizes the transformation of a part of nature into the altar on which Isaac is to be sacrificed. Even Isaac's name becomes an anagram of his fate: the Cyrillic letter 's' (which is shaped like the Latin 'c') mirrors the form of the victim – a sacrificial lamb with forelegs and hindlegs bound together.

There is a nightmarish section in *Gorbunov and Gorchakov* (Canto V) in which the Russian verb *skazal* ('he said') – in such phrases as *i on skazal* ('and he said') and *i on yemu skazal* ('and he said to him') – becomes thinglike and threatening, so like a thing as to take on the inflections of a Russian noun.

The same poem contains a remarkable meditation on the nature of speech and silence:

> '... silence is the future of all days
> that roll toward speech; yes, silence is the presence
> of farewells in our greetings as we touch.
> Indeed, the future of our words is silence –
> those words which have devoured the stuff of things.'

This passage culminates in the striking assertion:

> 'Life is but talk hurled in the face of silence.'

Brodsky's lines are occasionally a bit 'rough', his syntax a bit tangled, his images less than lucid. But all of his verse is marked by an impressive depth and energy, as well as an 'aggressiveness' of both meaning and style. Now thirty-two, he has been writing poetry for fourteen years. His poetic achievement during this brief period, and especially since 1962, bears comparison – in my considered judgement – with that of the thirty-two-year-old Anna Akhmatova (as of 1921), the thirty-two-year-old Boris Pasternak (as of

1922), and the thirty-two-year-old Marina Tsvetayeva and Osip Mandelstam (both as of 1924).

Whether Joseph Brodsky will one day stand beside these four giants of twentieth-century Russian poetry it is perhaps still too early to say. I myself am confident that he will.

GEORGE L. KLINE

A Note on the Translation

Like most Russian poets, Brodsky makes systematic use of rhyme. But, following Tsvetayeva and Pasternak, he adds to the store of perfect 'Pushkinian' rhymes numerous imperfect or slant rhymes, of two sorts: (1) slant rhymes, e.g., *krysham/slyshen, podvinsya/yedinstvo, Ariadny/varianty, tsitra/tsifra*; and (2) compound slant rhymes, in which a single polysyllabic word is rhymed with two or more monosyllables, e.g., *senovale/na vore, skryvali/ne vy li, tishe/ty zhe, gusto/vkus-to,* and (a rhyme involving both Latin and Russian words) *Vale/yedva li*. Some of Brodsky's rhyme schemes are *tours de force*. For example, most of *Gorbunov and Gorchakov* consists of ten-line stanzas with quintuple rhymes: *ababababab*; and *To a Certain Poetess* has eight-line stanzas with the rhyme scheme *aaabaaab*.

On the other hand, Brodsky has written a number of unrhymed 'sonnets', and some of his longer poems on 'Greek' themes are unrhymed, e.g., *A Halt in the Desert* and *Post Aetatem Nostram*. This is also true of a recent shorter poem, *Odysseus to Telemachus* (1972).

All of these translations preserve Brodsky's meters, but they use rhymes and slant-rhymes sparingly, and only in those cases where the rhymes can be introduced without 'padding'. Brodsky himself, in his brilliant translations of John Donne and Andrew Marvell, scrupulously reproduces both the metric pattern and the rhyme scheme of his originals. I wish that I could have done as much in putting Brodsky into English.

Earlier versions of a number of these translations were published in *Antaeus, Arroy, Boston After Dark, Mademoiselle,*

Nation, New Leader, New York Review of Books, Observer Review, Partisan Review, Russian Literature TriQuarterly, Russian Review, Saturday Review, Third Hour, TriQuarterly, Unicorn Journal, and *Works and Days.*

There remains the pleasant duty of expressing my deep appreciation for help generously provided at various stages in the making of these translations by Max Hayward, Vera Sandomirsky Dunham, A. Alvarez, Frances Lindley, Arcadi Nebolsine, and – most of all – Joseph Brodsky. I alone, of course, am responsible for whatever faults remain in these versions.

G.L.K.

Part 1

A Christmas Ballad

To Evgenii Rein, affectionately

In anguish unaccountable
the steady ship that burns at dark,
the small shy streetlamp of the night,
floats out of Alexander Park
in the exhaustion of dull bricks.
Like a pale-yellow, tiny rose,
it drifts along, past lovers' heads
and walkers' feet.[1]

In anguish unaccountable
sleep-walkers, drunkards, float like bees.
A stranger sadly snaps a shot
of the metropolis by night;
a cab with squeamish passengers
jolts loudly to Ordynka Street,[2]
and dead men stand in close embrace
with private homes.

In anguish unaccountable
a melancholy poet swims
along the town. Beside a shop
for kerosene, a porter stands,
round-faced and sad. A ladies' man,
now old, lopes down a dingy street.
A midnight wedding party sways
in anguish unaccountable.

On Moscow's murky south-side streets
a random swimmer sadly floats.
A Jewish accent wanders down

a yellowed melancholy stair.
A fragile beauty swims alone
from New Year's Eve to Saturday,[3]
exchanging love for bitterness,
unable to explain her grief.

The chilly evening floats above
our eyes; two trembling snowflakes strike
the bus. A pale and numbing wind
slaps reddened hands. The honey-gold
of evening-lamps flows out; a scent
of halvah fills the air. The Eve
of Christmas holds the pie of heaven
above its head.

Your New Year's Day floats on a wave,
within the city's purple sea,
in anguish unaccountable –
as though life will begin anew,
and we will live in fame and light
with sure success and bread to spare;
as though, from lurching to the left,
life will swing right.[4]

1962

1. Alexander Park lies next to the Kremlin on the side opposite the Lenin Mausoleum. Since its outer edge is below street level, its streetlights (which are shaped somewhat like ship's lanterns), though above the heads of people walking in the park itself, are below the feet of pedestrians on the sidewalk outside the park.

2. During several extended visits to Moscow the poetess Anna Akhmatova lived on Ordynka Street; Brodsky visited her there. This street, like the old Arbat, is known for its many small 'private' houses (*osobnyaki*).

3. New Year's Eve 1962 (31 December 1961) fell on a Sunday.

4. The terms 'left' and 'right' are not meant politically.

Sonnet

The month of January has flown past
the prison windows; I have heard the singing
of convicts in their labyrinth of cells:
'One of our brothers has regained his freedom.'
You still can hear the prisoners' low song,
the echoing footsteps of the wordless wardens.
And you yourself still sing, sing silently:
'Farewell, o January.'
Facing the window's light,
you swallow the warm air in giant gulps.
But I roam once again, sunk deep in thought,
down hallways, from the last interrogation
to the next one – toward that distant land
where there is neither March nor February.

1962

Exhaustion now is a more frequent guest,
and yet I speak less often of it now.
O, deeds of my domestic handicraft,
warm from the workshop of my rowdy soul,

what birds are you devising for yourself?
On whom will you bestow – or barter – them?
And must you live in nests of latest style
and sing in concert with the latest lyre?

Come back, my soul, and pluck a feather out,
the radio can croon to us of fame.
But tell me, soul, what was the look of life,
how did it stand up to your soaring glance?

Now, while the snow whirls – as if sprung entire
from nothingness – by the plain-corniced walls,
o street, draw me the silhouette of death,
and you, o bird, shriek out the shape of life.

For here I walk, and somewhere there you fly
no longer heedful of our mutterings;
for here I live, and somewhere there you cry,
beating your tremulous, translucent wings.

1960

You're coming home again. What does that mean?
Can there be anyone here who still needs you,
who would still want to count you as his friend?
You're home, you've bought sweet wine to drink with
   supper,

and, staring out the window, bit by bit
you come to see that *you're* the one who's guilty:
the only one. That's fine. Thank God for that.
Or maybe one should say, 'Thanks for small favors.'

It's fine that there is no one else to blame,
it's fine that you are free of all connections,
it's fine that in this world there is no one
who feels obliged to love you to distraction.

It's fine that no one ever took your arm
and saw you to the door on a dark evening,
it's fine to walk, alone, in this vast world
toward home from the tumultuous railroad station.

It's fine to catch yourself, while rushing home,
mouthing a phrase that's something less than candid;
you're suddenly aware that your own soul
is very slow to take in what has happened.

1961

Sonnet

Great-hearted Hector has been speared to death.
His soul is swimming through the darkened waters
where bushes rustle and white clouds go black.
The far sobs of Andromache are muted.

Now mighty Ajax, on this gloomy night,
wades knee-deep in the stream's transparent ripples,
and life runs out of his great, staring eyes
toward Hector. Ajax walks chest-deep. The darkness
has brimmed the deep well of his gaze; it stains
the bright warm waves, the restless underbrush.
The waters now have fallen to his waist;
his heavy sword, caught up by the swift stream,
sweeps out ahead
– and carries mighty Ajax in its wake.

1961

The tenant finds his new house wholly strange.
His quick glance trips on unfamiliar objects
whose shadows fit him so imperfectly
that they themselves are quite distressed about it.
But this house cannot stand its emptiness.
The lock alone – it seems somehow ungallant –
is slow to recognize the tenant's touch
and offers brief resistance in the darkness.
This present tenant is not like the old –
who moved a chest of drawers in, and a table,
thinking that he would never have to leave;
and yet he did: his dose of life proved fatal.
There's nothing, it would seem, that makes them one:
appearance, character, or psychic trauma.
And yet what's usually called 'a home'
is the one thing that these two have in common.

1962

The night-black sky shone brighter than his legs;
he could not drift into dissolving dark[1]

That evening, sprawling by an open fire,
we caught our first sight of the raven steed.

I have seen nothing in this world more black –
the very color of his limbs was coal.
His body was as black as emptiness,
blacker than night, from mane to trembling tail.
His flanks, which bore a blackness set apart,
had never known the saddle's bruising mark.
He stood unmoving, and he seemed to sleep.
But terror stalked the blackness of his hooves.

So black was he that shadows made no stain;
they could not dye him darker than he stood.
He was as black as any midnight dark
or any needle's fierce unfathomed heart –
as black as the dense trees that loom ahead,
as the tense void between the nested ribs,
the pit beneath the earth where a seed lies.
I know that here within us all is black –

and yet he gleamed still blacker to our gaze!
It was no more than midnight by my watch.
He came no closer by the slightest step.
Unplumbed obscurity lurked at his loins.
His back had wholly vanished from our sight;
no single spot of light now lingered there.

The whites of his two eyes struck like twin blows.
Their pupils were more terrifying still,

with the strange leer of eyes in negatives!
But why then did he interrupt his flight
to watch beside us till the morning dawned?
Why did he stand so close against the fire?
Why did he breathe the blackness of that air,
and crush the brittle bones of fallen leaves?
Why did he blaze black light from those great eyes?

– He sought to find a rider in our midst.

1961

 1. The two-line epigraph is Brodsky's and was written for this
poem.

The fire, as you can hear, is dying down.
The shadows in the corners have been shifting.
It's now too late to shake a fist at them
or yell at them to stop what they are doing.
This legion does not listen to commands.
It now has closed its ranks and forms a circle.
In silence it advances from the walls,
and I am suddenly at its dead center.
The bursts of darkness, like black question marks,
are mounting higher steadily and higher.
The dark drifts down more densely from above,
engulfs my chin, and crumples my white paper.
The clock hands have completely disappeared.
One cannot see them, and one cannot hear them.
There's nothing left but bright spots in one's eyes –
in eyes that now seem frozen and unmoving.
The fire has died. As you can hear, it's dead.
The bitter smoke swirls, clinging to the ceiling.
But this bright spot is stamped upon one's eyes.
Or rather it is stamped upon the darkness.

1962

Elegy for John Donne

John Donne has sunk in sleep . . . All things beside
are sleeping too: walls, bed, and floor – all sleep.
The table, pictures, carpets, hooks and bolts,
clothes-closets, cupboards, candles, curtains – all
now sleep: the washbowl, bottle, tumbler, bread,
breadknife and china, crystal, pots and pans,
bed-sheets and nightlamp, chests of drawers, a clock,
a mirror, stairway, doors. Night everywhere,
night in all things: in corners, in men's eyes,
in bed-sheets, in the papers on a desk,
in the worm-eaten words of sterile speech,
in logs and fire-tongs, in the blackened coals
of a dead fireplace – in each thing.
In undershirts, boots, stockings, shadows, shades
behind the mirror; in the backs of chairs,
in bed and washbowl, in the crucifix,
in linen, in the broom beside the door,
in slippers. All these things have sunk in sleep.
Yes, all things sleep. The window. Snow beyond.
A roof-slope, whiter than a tablecloth,
the roof's high ridge. A neighborhood in snow,
carved to the quick by this sharp windowframe.
Arches and walls and windows – all asleep.
Wood paving-blocks, stone cobbles, gardens, grills.
No light will flare, no turning wheel will creak . . .
Chains, walled enclosures, ornaments, and curbs.
Doors with their rings, knobs, hooks are all asleep –
their locks and bars, their bolts and cunning keys.
One hears no whisper, rustle, thump, or thud.
Only the snow creaks. All men sleep. Dawn comes

not soon. All jails and locks have lapsed in sleep.
The iron weights in the fish-shop are asleep.
The carcasses of pigs sleep too. Backyards
and houses. Watch-dogs in their chains lie cold.
In cellars sleeping cats hold up their ears.
Mice sleep, and men. And London soundly sleeps.
A schooner nods at anchor. The salt sea
talks in its sleep with snows beneath her hull,
and melts into the distant sleeping sky.
John Donne has sunk in sleep, with him the sea.
Chalk cliffs now tower in sleep above the sands.
This island sleeps, embraced by lonely dreams,
and every garden now is triple-barred.
Pines, maples, birches, firs, and spruce – all sleep.
On mountain slopes steep mountain-streams and paths
now sleep. Foxes and wolves. Bears in their dens.
The snow drifts high at burrow-entrances.
All the birds sleep. Their songs are heard no more.
Nor is the crow's hoarse *caw*. At night the owl's
dark hollow laugh is quenched. The open fields
of England now are stilled. A clear star flames.
The mice are penitent. All creatures sleep.
The dead lie calmly in their graves and dream.
The living, in the oceans of their gowns,
sleep – each alone – within their beds. Or two
by two. Hills, woods, and rivers sleep. All birds
and beasts now sleep – nature alive and dead.
But still the snow spins white from the black sky.
There, high above men's heads, all are asleep.
The angels sleep. Saints – to their saintly shame –
have quite forgotten this our anxious world.
Dark Hell-fires sleep, and glorious Paradise.
No one goes forth from home at this bleak hour.
Even God has gone to sleep. Earth is estranged.

Eyes do not see, and ears perceive no sound.
The Devil sleeps. Harsh enmity has fallen
asleep with him on snowy English fields.
All horsemen sleep.[1] And the Archangel, with
his trumpet. Horses, softly swaying, sleep.
And all the cherubim, in one great host
embracing, doze beneath St Paul's high dome.
John Donne has sunk in sleep. His verses sleep.
His images, his rhymes, and his strong lines
fade out of view. Anxiety and sin,
alike grown slack, sleep in his syllables.
And each verse whispers to its next of kin,
'Move on a bit.' But each stands so remote
from Heaven's Gates, so poor, so pure and dense,
that all seems one. All are asleep. The vault
austere of iambs soars in sleep. Like guards,
the trochees stand and nod to left and right.
The vision of Lethean waters sleeps.
The poet's fame sleeps soundly at its side.
All trials, all sufferings, are sunk in sleep.
And vices sleep. Good lies in Evil's arms.
The prophets sleep. The bleaching snow seeks out,
through endless space, the last unwhitened spot.
All things have lapsed in sleep. The swarms of books,
the streams of words, cloaked in oblivion's ice,
sleep soundly. Every speech, each speech's truth,
is sleeping. Linked chains, sleeping, scarcely clank.
All soundly sleep: the saints, the Devil, God.
Their wicked and their faithful servants. Snow
alone sifts, rustling, on the darkened roads.
And there are no more sounds in all the world.

But hark! Do you not hear in the chill night
a sound of sobbing, whisperings of fear?

There someone stands, disclosed to winter's blast,
and weeps. There someone stands in the dense gloom.
His voice is thin. His voice is needle-thin,
yet without thread. And he in solitude
swims through the falling snow – cloaked in cold mist –
that stitches night to dawn. The lofty dawn.
'Whose sobs are those? My angel, is it you?
Do you await my coming, there alone
beneath the snow? Walking – without my love –
in darkness home? Do you cry in the gloom?'
No answer. – 'Is it you, o cherubim,
whose muted tears put me in mind
of some sepulchral choir? Have you resolved
to quit my sleeping church? Is it not you?'
No answer. – 'Is it you, o Paul? Your voice
most certainly is coarsened by stern speech.
Have you not bowed your grey head in the gloom
to weep?' But only silence makes reply.
'Is that the Hand which looms up everywhere
to shield a grieving glance in the deep dark?
Is it not thou, Lord? No, my thought runs wild.
And yet how lofty is the voice that weeps.'
No answer. Silence. – 'Gabriel, have you
not blown your trumpet to the roar of hounds?
Why did I stand alone with open eyes
while horsemen saddled their swift steeds? Yet each
thing sleeps. Enveloped in huge gloom, the Hounds
of Heaven race in packs. O Gabriel,
do you not sob, encompasséd about
by winter dark, alone, with your great horn?'

'No, it is I, your soul, John Donne, who speaks.
I grieve alone upon the heights of Heaven,
because my labors did bring forth to life

feelings and thoughts as heavy as stark chains.
Bearing this burden, you could yet fly up
past those dark sins and passions, mounting higher.
You were a bird, your people did you see
in every place, as you did soar above
their sloping roofs. And you did glimpse the seas,
and distant lands, and Hell – first in your dreams,
then waking. You did see a jewelled Heaven
set in the wretched frame of men's low lusts.
And you saw Life: your Island was its twin.
And you did face the ocean at its shores.
The howling dark stood close at every hand.
And you did soar past God, and then drop back,
for this harsh burden would not let you rise
to that high vantage point from which this world
seems naught but ribboned rivers and tall towers –
that point from which, to him who downward stares,
this dread Last Judgement seems no longer dread.
The radiance of that Country does not fade.
From there all here seems a faint, fevered dream.
From there our Lord is but a light that gleams,
through fog, in window of the farthest house.
The fields lie fallow, furrowed by no plough.
The years lie fallow, and the centuries.
Forests alone stand, like a steady wall.
Rain batters the high head of giant grass.
The first woodcutter – he whose withered mount,
in panic fear of thickets, blundered thence –
will climb a pine to catch a sudden glimpse
of fires in his own valley, far away.
All things are distant. What is near is dim.
The level glance slides from a roof remote.
All here is bright. No din of baying hound
or tolling bell disturbs the silent air.

And, sensing that all things are far away,
he'll wheel his horse back quickly toward the woods.
And instantly, reins, sledge, night, his poor mount,
himself – will melt into a Scriptural dream.
But here I stand and weep. The road is gone.
I am condemned to live among these stones.
I cannot fly up in my body's flesh;
such flight at best will come to me through death
in the wet earth, when I've forgotten you,
my world, forgotten you once and for all.
I'll follow, in the torment of desire,
to stitch this parting up with my own flesh.
But listen! While with weeping I disturb
your rest, the busy snow whirls through the dark,
not melting, as it stitches up this hurt –
its needles flying back and forth, back, forth!
It is not I who sob. It's you, John Donne:
you lie alone. Your pans in cupboards sleep,
while snow builds drifts upon your sleeping house –
while snow sifts down to earth from highest Heaven.'

Like some great bird, he sleeps in his own nest,
his pure path and his thirst for purer life,
himself entrusting to that steady star
which now is closed in clouds. And like a bird,
his soul is pure, and his life's path on earth,
although it needs must wind through sin, is still
closer to nature than that tall crow's nest
which soars above the starlings' empty homes.
Like some great bird, he too will wake at dawn;
but now he lies beneath a veil of white,
while snow and sleep stitch up the throbbing void
between his soul and his own dreaming flesh.
All things have sunk in sleep. But one last verse

awaits its end, baring its fangs to snarl
that carnal love is but a poet's duty –
spiritual love the essence of a priest.
Whatever millstone these swift waters turn
will grind the same coarse grain in this one world.
For though our life may be a thing to share,
who is there in this world to share our death?
Man's garment gapes with holes. It can be torn,
by him who will, at this edge or at that.
It falls to shreds and is made whole again.
Once more it's rent. And only the far sky,
in darkness, brings the healing needle home.
Sleep, John Donne, sleep. Sleep soundly, do not fret
your soul. As for your coat, it's torn; all limp
it hangs. But see, there from the clouds will shine
that Star which made your world endure till now.

1963

1. The allusion is both to the English knights who fought in the
Wars of the Roses and to the Four Horsemen of the Apocalypse.

Sonnet

To G. P.

Once more we're living by the Bay of Naples;[1]
and clouds of black smoke drift, daily, above us.
Our own Vesuvius has cleared its throat;
volcanic ash is settling in the side-streets.
Our windowpanes have rattled to its roaring.
Some day we too will be shrouded with ashes.

And when that happens, at that awful moment,
I'd like to take a streetcar to the outskirts
of town and find your house;
and if, after a thousand years,
a swarm of scientists should come here
to dig our city out, I hope they'll find me,
cloaked with the ashes of our modern epoch,
and everlastingly within your arms.

1962

1. The Russian *zaliv* ('bay' or 'gulf') could refer to the Gulf of
Finland, on which Leningrad is located. But the reference to Vesuvius
makes it clear that the Bay of Naples is also intended.

Part 2

To M. B.

When I embraced these shoulders, I beheld
the room as it was now revealed beyond us.
I saw how a straight chair pushed from the wall
had blended with the brilliant glow behind it.
The huge bulb in the lamp was far too strong –
its fierce glare made worn furniture look hollow;
the threadbare cover of the sofa shone
so greenly brown as to seem almost yellow.
The table stood deserted, and the floor
lay gleaming, while the stove seemed dark; a dusty
wood frame held a stiff landscape. The sideboard
appeared to be alone among the living.
A moth, aflutter in this empty blaze,
shook my fixed stare out of its frozen orbit.[1]
If any ghost had tried to haunt this place,
he must have left, for surely he abhorred it.

1962

1. *Moi vzglyad s nedvizhimosti sdvinul*, literally, 'shifted my gaze
away from the non-movable property'. However, the word *ne-
dvizhimost* also suggests immobility in general; hence the translation
as 'frozen orbit'.

Enigma for an Angel

To M. B.

Dreams rock the blanket-universe.
But someone strains to see the ocean;
it looms in the black night, sliced off
by sharp knives of the window casing.
The shrubs have trapped a moon-balloon.
Rowboats are sunk in conversation;
they say the bright shoes in this room
will never crush the shells of oysters.

A hand that holds a pillow fast
is creeping down a polished bedpost,
making its way to a cloud breast
by this inept and tongue-tied gesture.
A sock, torn on a jagged rock,
twists in the dark; its curve is swan-like.
Its funnel mouth is all agog;
it stares up like a blackened fishnet.

The wall helps us to have two seas
(perhaps we're helped by hazy thinking),
divided up in such a way
that two dark nets, which still hang empty,
at depths that one can scarcely plumb,
wait to be dragged up to the surface
by double lines lashed to the bars
that form a cross in the wide window.

A star glows yellow on the waves;
the rowboats loom, bereft of motion.
Framed in the window, the great cross

slowly revolves, like a winch turning.
The two nets move at steady pace
from empty depths up to the surface;
they hope that the revolving cross
will pull them in and cast them elsewhere.

All this takes place without a sound.
The empty window still is hopeful,
despite the house's fixity,
that the next net will come in loaded.
The window[1] in this dark night sees
(the moon has made its whole world brighter)
how flower beds roll in like waves,
and front-yard shrubs crash down like breakers.

The house is motionless, the fence
dives in the dark, with its bright cork-floats;
a hatchet stuck in the front steps
keeps its sharp eye on the wet dock-posts.
A clock is chattering. Far off
the grumbling of a speedboat's motor
drowns out the crunch of oyster shells
stamped under by a fleshless walker.

Two eyes emit a piercing scream.
The eyelids close, with a vague rustle,
like oyster shells curved in the gloom
to cover and protect the pupil.
How long until this pain is gone,
swamped by the talk of outboard motors,
to break out then on a warm arm
as pale scars of a vaccination?

How long? Till morning? Surely not.
The wind attempts, with a faint murmur,

to lift the jasmine veil that blocks
the open face of the blank gateway.[2]
The nets are all hauled in. A screech
piped by a hoopoe-bird has headed
off would-be thieves. On the dark beach
the walker, wordless still, has faded.

1962

1. In Russian the connection between 'window' (*okno*) and 'eye' (in Old Slavic *oko*) is somewhat more evident than in English.

2. These three lines are translated from an unpublished variant supplied by the poet.

A Slice of Honeymoon

To M. B.

Never, never forget:
how the waves lashed the docks,
and the wind pressed upward
like submerged life-buoys.

– How the seagulls chattered,
sailboats stared at the sky.
– How the clouds swooped upwards
like wild ducks flying.

May this tiny fragment
of the life we then shared
beat in your heart wildly
like a fish not yet dead.

May the bushes bristle.
May the oysters snap.
May the passion cresting
at your lips make you grasp

– without words – how the surf
of these breaking waves
brings fresh crests to birth
in the open sea.

1963

To M. B.

You'll flutter, robin redbreast, from those three
raspberry bushes, thus – in my unfreedom –
recalling how the thick-napped lupin field
at dusk invades the tranquil green-pea kingdom.
You'll flutter through the closely packed moustache
of pussywillows, where countless dew droplets,
their tiny hearts stunned by the sudden shock,
will cascade down the green slopes of the pea-pods.

Spasms will rack the raspberry bush, yet
a riddle lingers. It may just have happened:
some hunter, as he lays his trap, has stepped
incautiously and sets a dead branch crackling.
In fact, only a thin ribbon of path
twists through the darkness, ashen white and serious;
unheard here: gurgling, or a rifle shot –
unseen: Aquarius, or Sagittarius.[1]

The night moves on inverted wings, aloft,
above dense bushes that now hang upside-down –
insistent, like the memory of the past,
a silent past that seems somehow to live on.

24 May 1964[2]

1. These two constellations are not visible at the latitude of the
Arkhangelsk region where this poem was written.
2. The date is Brodsky's twenty-fourth birthday.

A Prophecy

We'll go and live together by the shore;
huge dams will wall us from the continent.
A home-made lamp will hurl its warming glow
across the roundness of our centered space.
We shall wage war at cards, and cock an ear
to catch the crashing of the maddened surf.
We'll gently cough, or sigh a soundless sigh,
whenever the wind roars too raucously.

I shall be old, and you will still be young.
But, as the youngsters say, we'll count the time
that's left us till the new age breaks in days,
not years. In our reversed, small Netherland[1]
we'll plant a kitchen-garden, you and I;
and we shall sizzle oysters by the door,
and drink the rays of the sun's octopus,

Let summer rains crash on our cucumbers;
we'll get as tanned as any Eskimo,
and you will run your fingers tenderly
along the virgin V where I'm unburned.[2]
I'll see my collarbone in the clear glass,
and glimpse a mirrored wave behind my back,
and my old Geiger counter, cased in tin,
that dangles from its faded, sweat-soaked strap.

When winter comes, unpitying, it will
twist off the thatch from our wood roof. And if
we make a child, we'll call the boy Andrei,
Anna the girl, so that our Russian speech,

imprinted on its wrinkled little face,
shall never be forgot. Our alphabet's
first sound is but the lengthening of a sigh
and thus may be affirmed for future time.

We shall wage war at cards until the tide's
retreating sinuosities draw us,
with all our trumps, down and away ...
Our child will gaze in silence at a moth,
not fathoming its urgent moth-motives
for beating at our lamp. But then the time
will come when he must make his way back through
the dam that walls us from the continent.

1965

1. The 'Netherland' is 'reversed' in the sense that it lies on the *sea* side of the dam. The latter serves as a barrier not against the sea but against the mainland, with its threat of atomic devastation.
2. The V-shaped area on chest and collarbones shielded from the sun's rays by the strap of the Geiger counter.

New Stanzas to Augusta[1]

To M. B.

I

September came on Tuesday.
It poured all night.
The birds had all flown south.
I was so much alone, so brave,
I did not even watch them go.
The empty sky is broken now.
Rain-curtains close the last clear spot.
I need no south.

II

Buried alive here,
I wade through twilight stubble.
My boots churn up the field
(Thursday blusters above my head),
but the cut stalks stand erect,
feeling almost no pain.
Switches of pussywillow
plunge a pinkish headland
into the swamp where the guard has been lifted,
muttering something as they upset
a nest of shrikes.

III

Beat and slosh, swirl and gurgle.
I do not quicken my steps.
O God, snuff out
the spark that thou alone dost know.
My frozen hands pressed to my hips,
I roam from mound to hillock –

without memories, with only an inner noise,
kicking my bootsoles against the rocks.
I bend down over a dark stream,
and recoil in shock.

IV
What does it matter that a shadow of mindlessness
has crossed my eyes, that the damp
has soaked my beard, that my cap, askew,
– a crown for this twilight – is reflected
like some boundary beyond which
my soul cannot penetrate?
I do not try to get beyond my visor,
buttons, collar, boots, or cuffs.
But my heart pounds suddenly when I discover
that somewhere I am torn. The cold
crashes into my chest, jolting my heart.

V
The water mutters ahead of me,
and the frost reaches out for the slit of my mouth.
With more than a slit one cannot breathe:
but is this a face, or the scene
of a landslide?
My laugh is twisted;
it brings terror to the brushwood path
that cuts across the twilight swamp.
A gust of rain atomizes the darkness.
My shadow runs, like a thing alive,
from these reddened eyelids, galloping
on waveback under pines and weeping willows.
It loses itself among its shadowy doubles
as I could never do.

VI

Beat and slosh. Chew into the rotted bridge.
The swampy soil around the country churchyard
sucks the blue color from the wooden crosses.
But even the leaves of grass
cannot give this swamp a tinge of blue.
Trample the oat bins,
rage through the still-thick foliage.
Penetrate to the root depths
and rouse all the dead men, all the ghosts,
there, in the earth, and here, in my heart.
Let them escape, cutting corners as they run,
across the stubble, into the emptied villages;
let them wave their scarecrow hats to greet
arriving autumn days – abrupt like landed birds.

VII

Here on the hills, under empty skies,
among roads which end in forests,
life steps back from itself
and stares astonished at its own
hissing and roaring forms.
Roots cling, wheezing, to your boots,
and no lights show in the whole village.
Here I wander in a no-man's land
and take a lease on non-existence.
Wind tears the warmth out of my hands.
A tree-hollow douses me with water;
mud twists the ribbon of the footpath.

VIII

It's as though I'm not really here,
but somewhere on the sidelines, somewhere overboard.
The stubble swells and points straight up

like a corpse's beard;
on the shrike's nest that lies in the grass
a riot of ants boils with indignation.
Nature settles its accounts with the past
in the same old way. But her face,
even when flooded with sunset light,
betrays her malice.
With all five of my senses
I shove off from the forest.
No, Lord! My eyes are clouded;
I shall not sit in judgement.
And if – to my misfortune –
I prove unable to control myself,
o God, hack off all of my senses,
like the five fingers of a thieving Finn.[2]

IX

Pollux, dear friend. All merges to a stain.
No groan shall be wrenched from my lips.
Here I stand, my coat thrown open,
letting the world flow into my eyes
through a sieve of incomprehension.
I'm nearly deaf, o God. I'm nearly blind.
I hear no words, and the moon burns steadily
at no more than twenty watts. I will not set
my course across the sky between the stars
and raindrops. The woods will echo
not with my songs, but only with my coughs.

X

September now. And night. My only
company a candle. But a shadow
peers over my shoulder at these papers,
swarming among the torn-up roots.

exile

gelsk.

The title refers to Byron's
translated into Russian): ir
woman who remains behi
'M. B.', to whom this po
   2. It was once the cust
victed thief.

An apparition of you rustles
among the shadows, gurgling in the water,
smiling starlike in the open doorway.

XI

The light fades out above my head.
The water covers up my tracks.

Yes, this heart rushes toward you –
harder and harder, farther and farther.
A falser and falser note creeps into my voice.
But you will set this down to fate,
a fate which does not ask for blood
but wounds me with a blunted needle.
And if you're hoping for a smile –
just wait, I'll smile! My smile will float
above me like the grave's long-standing
roof, lighter than woodsmoke.

XII

Euterpe, is it you? Where am I?
What's this beneath me: water, grass,
the offshoot of a lyre of heather-boughs,
curved to a horseshoe shape, that seems
to promise happiness. But neither you
nor your Calliope
knows how to change the pace
of a man's life – slowing from run to walk –
without breaking the rhythm of his breath.

1964

1. This poem was written during the first year of Brodsky's exile
in a remote northern region of Russia: the province of Arkhangelsk.

The title refers to Byron's 'Stanzas to Augusta' (which Pasternak had translated into Russian): in both cases an exiled poet addresses a loved woman who remains behind – in Byron's case, his sister; in Brodsky's, 'M. B.', to whom this poem is dedicated.

2. It was once the custom in Finland to cut off the hand of a convicted thief.

To Lycomedes on Scyros

I quit this city, as once Theseus quit
the labyrinth, leaving the Minotaur
to rot, and Ariadne to make love
with Bacchus.
              Such, they say, is victory!
An apotheosis of moral virtue.
But God has so arranged it that we meet
at just that moment when, our exploit done
within the city, we now wander, big
with booty, through vast vacant lots and leave
this place, intending never to return.

When all is said and done, a murder is
a murder. And we mortals have a duty
to take up arms against all monsters. Who
maintains that monsters are immortal? God
in secret – lest we pridefully assume
ourselves to be distinct from those we've vanquished –
subtracts all recompense at a remove
from the exultant mob. And bids us hold
our tongues. And so we fade away.

This time, indeed, we go for good. Men can
return to where they have done evil deeds,
but men do not return to where they've been
abased. On this point God's design and our
own feeling of abasement coincide
so absolutely that we quit: the night,
the rotting beast, the exultant mob, our homes,

our hearthfires, Bacchus in a vacant lot
embracing Ariadne in the dark.

But one day we must all go back. Back home.
Back to our native hearth. And my own path
lies through this city's heart. God grant that I
shall not have with me then a two-edged sword –
since cities start, for those who dwell in them,
with central squares and towers –
                              but for the wanderer
approaching –
                  with their outskirts.

1967

Refusing to catalogue all of one's woes
is a very broad gesture in pedants!
Contracting all space to the size of those spots
where I've crawled in the pain of existence,
as a tailor who's drunk and is raging toward death
sews a patch on a nobleman's garment –
so I cast my long spell on your fast-moving life
from the seamy side of your horizons!

The alleys and suburbs, backyards, vacant lots,
and fences – wherever you've wandered,
whatever you've chosen to make up your life:
I've known it so well that the backdrop
of our little tragedy – where our love died –
will seem both unlovely and sterile –
wherever you happen to set up the bed
of your love – like the famous Blood Temple.[1]

So take my percentage and buy wedding doves
with cash from our bleak separation.
As amputees drink to their stumps, so I'll raise
my glass to a past that was better.
You've put away crutches to life's varied ends;
accept all of life without flinching:
your bed, built on gossip,[2] is surely as hard
as mine on the calendar's margin.

Even dead, I shall mean more to you and your life
than hills or the lake and the river.
The earth can reveal nothing more of the truth

than what your own eyes can discover.
Behind you each blade of the downtrodden grass
springs up like a nondescript rooster.
The circles will widen, like loops of a gaze
that rolls after you while miles reduce you.

A stunned fish that surfaces from the stream's depths,
a wandering ghost at interments,
a body that rots in its clean winding sheets:
my shade, vying with the bright heavens,
will everywhere loudly proclaim to your ears
that I am a full-fledged messiah,
whose body will writhe in your sight on each wall
of that house whose high roof is called 'Russia'.

June 1967

1. 'Blood Temple' (*khram na krovi*) – a reference to the *Khram voskreseniya na krovi* (literally, 'Temple of the Resurrection on Blood'), a somewhat garish pseudo-Byzantine church, modelled on St Basil's in Moscow, which was built in St Petersburg on the spot where Alexander II was assassinated in 1881.
2. An allusion to a line in Pasternak's *Smert poeta* ('Death of a Poet'), written on the occasion of Mayakovsky's suicide in 1930: *ty spal, postlav postel na spletne* ('you slept, having made your bed on gossip').

Stanzas[1]

I

Let our farewell be silent.
Turn the phonograph down.
Separations in this world
hint at partings beyond.
It's not just in this lifetime
that we must sleep apart.
Death won't bring us together
or wipe out our love's hurt.

II

And whichever is guilty,
when the Last Judgement sounds,
will receive no such welcome
as the innocent one.
Our farewell's the more final
since we both are aware
that we'll not meet in Heaven
or be neighbors in Hell.

III

As a plough cuts the humus,
the fact we've both been
in the right cuts between us
more completely than sin.
We are careless, not guilty
when we knock a glass down.
What's the good, once it's broken,
weeping over spilt wine?

IV

As our union was perfect,
so our break is complete.
Neither panning nor zooming
can postpone the fade-out.
There's no point in our claiming
that our fusion's still real.
But a talented fragment
can pretend to be whole.

V

Swoon, then, to o'erflowing,
drain yourself till you're dry.
We two halves share the volume,
not the strength, of the wine.
But my world will not end if
in future we share
only those jagged edges
where we've broken apart.

VI

No man stands as a stranger.
But the threshold of shame
is defined by our feelings
at the 'Never again'.
Thus, we mourn, yet we bury,
and resume our concerns,
cutting death at its center
like two clear synonyms.

VII

That we can't be together
anywhere in this realm
makes it one variation

on a vast cosmic theme.
Our own land envies glory
yet it yields to no power
on the far side of Lethe
in its naked and poor.

VIII
Why then these vain efforts
to wipe out what has been?
These poor lines can but echo
the disaster we've known.
This mushrooming gossip
supplies added proof
that starts are less noted
than endings of love.

IX
Let our farewell be silent
so that our split address
(yours is 'angel', mine 'devil')
may invite no caress
from the fierce Hounds of Heaven.
Choired muses will grieve,
since our posthumous torments
bring harsh pain while we live.

March 1968

1. Brodsky considerably shortened this poem in 1972, deleting
Stanzas VII and IX of the original version. This translation is based on
the shortened text.

Aeneas and Dido

The great man stared out through the open window;
but her entire world ended at the border
of his broad Grecian tunic, whose abundance
of folds had the fixed, frozen look of seawaves
long since immobilized.
                   And he still stared
through the wide window with a gaze so distant
that his lips seemed to freeze and form a seashell,
one that concealed an inward, muted roar.
The shimmering horizon in his goblet
was motionless.
               But her vast love appeared
to be only a fish, a fish which yet
might plunge into the sea after his ship,
knifing the waves with its slim supple body,
and somehow overtake him – except that he,
in thought, already strode upon dry land.
The sea became a sea of shining tears.
But, as we know, precisely at the moment
when our despair is deepest, fresh winds stir.
The great man sailed from Carthage.
                  Dido stood
alone before the bonfire which her soldiers
had kindled by the city walls, and there –
as in a vision trembling between flame
and smoke – she watched great Carthage silently
crumble to ash,

long ages before Cato's prophecy.

1969

Postscriptum

How sad that my life has not come to mean
for you what your life came to mean for me.
... How many times in vacant lots have I
consigned my copper coin, crowned with the seal
of state, to that webbed universe of wires,
attempting hopelessly to stretch the time
of our connectedness ... Alas, unless
a man can manage to eclipse the world,
he's left to twirl a gap-toothed dial in some
phone booth, as one might spin a ouija board,
until a phantom answers, echoing
the last wails of a buzzer in the night.

September 1967

Part 3

Quilt-jacketed, a tree-surgeon
hopped, thrush-like, from a ladder-step
to a high limb, throwing a bridge
twixt bipeds: 'feather-less' and '-ed'.

But, instead of a chirping song
one heard the scraping sound of man;
blade clashed on blade, as shivers ran
down my tense spine and up again.

It's here that featherless bipeds
reveal that they are worlds apart
(much more than by their high-domed heads)
from feathered bipeds and their art.

When we unclose our beak-like shears
in winter trees, we click and squeak;
but we produce no arias.
Are we not lower than these 'beasts'?

Taking the product of their nests,
their brief lives and the way they sing
in total self-forgetfulness –
we can define our lesser range.

18 January 1964

Wagon Train

The thicker the shadows spill,
the farther the wagons roll
from the pain of these stubbled fields –
the louder their axles squeal.
They stagger from rut to rut.
The thicker the foliage gets,
the more the flat meadows fade –
the louder the wagons bray.

The bare tips of alder trees
and yellow-birch brushes see –
when they have stopped shivering –
how bound sheaves glance longingly
at the free sweep of open sky.
Once more something snags the wheels:
the trees cannot hear bird-chirps,
but only the wood-spokes' screech,
the drivers' quarrelsome speech.

Tarusa, February 1964

Sadly and Tenderly[1]

To A. Gorbunov

They served us noodles one more time, and you,
Mickiewicz, pushing back the soup-bowl, said
that you would rather eat nothing at all.
Hence I, too, without risk that the attendant
would think me mutinous, could follow you
to the latrine and stay there till retreat.
'The month of January always yields
to February, then comes March.' Thin scraps
of conversation. Tiles and porcelain
aglow, where water makes a crystal sound.

Mickiewicz lay down, his unseeing eyes
fixed on the orange nightlamp by the door.
(Perhaps he saw his own fate mirrored there.)
Babanov called the attendant to the hall.
Beside the darkened window I stood rooted;
behind my back the television crackled.
'Hey, Gorbunov, just look at that huge tail.' –
'And that queer eye.' – 'And there, see that big lump
above the fin.' – 'It seems to be an abscess.'
Thus, mouths agape and goggle-eyed, we stared
through winter[2] windows at the starry Fish[3]
and wagged our shaven heads, in that place where
men spit on floors –

where sometimes we are given fish to eat,
but never knife or fork to eat it with.

1964

1. The scene is the 'special' psychiatric prison hospital in Leningrad in which Brodsky spent a brief period undergoing psychiatric examination prior to his trial, which began in February 1964.
2. Literally, 'in February'.
3. The constellation Pisces.

Spring Season of Muddy Roads

The rain has turned the roads
to rivers.
I load an oar aboard
the wagon.
I've oiled the horse-collar,
a life-vest.[1]
Just for emergencies.
I'm prudent.

The road's as stubborn as
the river.
The ashtree's shadow is
a fishnet.
My horse won't taste his dish
of mud-soup.
The chortling wheels reject
it flatly.

It's not quite spring, but some-
thing like it.
The world is scattered now,
and crooked.
The ragged villages
are limping.
There's straightness only in
bored glances.

The hazel branches scratch
the wagon.

My horse's snout touches
his life-vest.
Above my dapple-gray's
splashed withers
eight giant cranes are fly-
ing northward.

Look at me, here, o friend,
o future:
well-armed with harness ribs
and traces,
half-way along the road
to nature –
in my twenty-fifth year –
I'm singing.

1964

1. The Russian word for 'life-vest' is *spasatelny krug*, literally 'saving circle'. Brodsky punningly describes the horse-collar as a *spasatelny oval*, literally 'saving oval'.

In villages God does not live only
in icon corners, as the scoffers claim,
but plainly, everywhere. He sanctifies
each roof and pan, divides each double door.
In villages God acts abundantly –
cooks lentils in iron pots on Saturdays,
dances a lazy jig in flickering flames,
and winks at me, witness to all of this.
He plants a hedge, and gives away a bride
(the groom's a forester), and, for a joke,
he makes it certain that the game warden
will never hit the duck he's shooting at.

The chance to know and witness all of this,
amidst the whistling of the autumn mist,
is, I would say, the only touch of bliss
that's open to a village atheist.

1964

The days glide over me
like clouds over the treetops,
merged into a white herd
at the back of the forest.

Fixed above the cold streams –
without cowbells, or mooing –
the days press their huge frames
on the fence of the cow-pen.

This horizon of hills
breathes no word of escaping.
And sometimes the fresh dawn
leaves no trace of what-has-been.

In their transit through time
evenings speedily voyage
far above starling-homes,
far beyond the black tillage.

June 1964

To M. B.

The trees in my window, in my wooden-framed window,
double their ranks after rain, surrounding
the village – by means of bright puddles –
with a reinforced guard of dead souls.

These trees have no earth under them; but I,
like some new Chichikov,[1] setting my mind on doubling,
find their leaves in the skies
and my reflection in your eyes.

This upside-down forest gives me my full due,
rummaging with both hands at the bottom of each puddle.

A boat, afloat on dry land, bounces on the waves.
The ranks of the trees, in my wooden-framed window,
   are doubled.

October 1964

   1. Chichikov is the hero (or 'anti-hero') of Gogol's *Dead Souls*.

Now that I've walled myself off from the world,
I'd like to wall myself off from myself.
Not fences of hewn poles, but mirror glass,
it seems to me, will best accomplish this.
I'll study the dark features of my face:
my bristly beard, the blotches on my chin.
Perhaps there is no better kind of wall
than a three-faced mirror for this parted pair.[1]
This mirror shows, in twilight from the door,
huge starlings at the edge of the ploughland,
and lakes like breaches in the wall, yet crowned
with fir-tree teeth.
                          Behold, the world beyond
creeps through these lakes – these breaches in our world –
indeed, through every puddle opening.
Or else this world crawls through them to the sky.

1966

1. The 'parted pair' is the poet and his own reflection, **from which** he has been 'separated' by his mirror.

Evening

Snow had sifted through cracks
and soft-powdered the hay.
When I scattered the stalks
I could see a moth stir.
Little moth, little moth!
You staved off your death,
creeping into this loft:
hibernated, survived.

The moth lived to see how
my lantern[1] made smoke trails,
and how brightly lit up
were the planks of the walls.
When I held him up close
I could see his antennas –
more clearly than the flame
or my own two cupped hands.

We are wholly alone
in the evening gloom.
And my fingers are warm
like the lost days of June.

1965

1. The *letuchaya mysh* (literally, 'bat') is a box-like Russian lantern, having four glass sides which enclose a candle.

1 January 1965¹

The Wise Men will unlearn your name.
Above your head no star will flame.
One weary sound will be the same –
the hoarse roar of the gale.
The shadows fall from your tired eyes
as your lone bedside candle dies,
for here the calendar breeds nights
till stores of candles fail.

What prompts this melancholy key?
A long familiar melody.
It sounds again. So let it be.
Let it sound from this night.
Let it sound in my hour of death –
as gratefulness of eyes and lips
for that which sometimes makes us lift
our gaze to the far sky.

You glare in silence at the wall.
Your stocking gapes: no gifts at all.
It's clear that you are now too old
to trust in good Saint Nick;
that it's too late for miracles.
– But suddenly, lifting your eyes
to heaven's light, you realize:
your *life* is a sheer gift.

1965

1. Brodsky often refers to this as his 'Christmas poem'. Christmas falls on 6 January in the Russian Orthodox calendar. In the Soviet Union gifts are usually exchanged on New Year's Day.

The Candlestick

The satyr, having quit the bronzy stream,
gripped the tall candelabra with six stems
as though it were a thing that he possessed.
But, as the inventory puts it, sternly,
he is a thing possessed by it. Alas,
all forms of ownership are such as this.
The satyr's no exception. Thus it is
the oxide on his scrotum glimmers greenly.

Fancy accentuates the waking world.
It happened thus: he swam across the stream
into whose mirror the high candle-tree
had put down its six limbs – with a soft burbling.
He clasped the trunk, but found that it was marked
as a possession of the earth. Behind
his back the stream wiped out his tracks. Its bed
was through-shine bright. And philomel was warbling.

If this had lasted just one moment more
the satyr would have won his solitude,
proving that stream and earth could do without him;
but in that final moment his mind slackened.
The world went black. But mirrors in each corner
repeated the glad tidings, 'He yet lives.'
The candlestick stood crowned upon the table,
charming each witness with attained perfection.

Not death, but a new setting, waits for us.
The satyr had nothing to fear from bronze-like
photographs. Crossing his Rubicon,

he became metal – locks to genitals.
It seems that what art strives for is to be
precise and not to tell us lies, because
its fundamental law undoubtedly
asserts the independence of details.

So light the candles then! Stop chattering
about illuminating someone's twilight.
No one of us is sovereign over others,
although to such ill-omened thoughts we cling.
It's not for me, fair maiden, to embrace you,
nor for you to reproach me, tearfully.
Since candle-wax, my dear, lights up the world
of things themselves, not the bare thoughts of things.

1968

On Washerwoman Bridge[1]

On Washerwoman Bridge, where you and I
stood like the two hands of a midnight clock
embracing, soon to part, not for a day
but for all days – this morning on our bridge
a narcissistic fisherman,
forgetting his cork float, stares goggle-eyed
at his unsteady river image.

The ripples age him and then make him young;
a web of wrinkles flows across his brow
and melts into the features of his youth.
He holds our place. Why not? – It is his right.
In recent years whatever stands alone
stands as a symbol of another time.
His is a claim for space.
                    So let him gaze
into our waters, calmly, at himself,
and even come to know himself. The river
is his by right today. It's like a house
in which new tenants have set up a mirror
but have not yet moved in.

1968

1. The *Prachechny Most* is a well-known bridge across the Fontanka
River in Leningrad at the site of the former Imperial Laundry.

September the First

The day was called, simply, 'September first'.
The Fall had come; the children were at school.
At Poland's border, Germans raised striped bars.
Their roaring tanks, like fingernails that smooth
the tinfoil on a piece of chocolate,
flattened the uhlan lancers.
                              Set out glasses!
We'll drink a toast to those uhlans who stood
in first place on the roster of the dead,
as on a classroom roster.
                              Once again
the birches rustle in the wind; dead leaves
sift down on the low roofs of houses where
no children's voices sound, as though on fallen
Polish caps.[1] The rumbling clouds crawl past,
avoiding the dead eyes of sunset windows.

1967

1. The Polish *konfederatka*: a military cap with a square roof-like
top.

The Fountain

From the lion's jaws
no stream ripples, no roar sounds.
Hyacinths bloom. There is no whistle, no cry,
no voice at all. The leaves are motionless.
This is a strange setting for so threatening a visage,
a new setting.
His lips are parched,
his throat has rusted through: metal is not deathless.
The faucet has been turned completely off,
the faucet which lies hidden in bushes at the end of his tail.
A nettle has clogged the valve. Evening descends;
from among the shrubs
a swarm of shadows
runs headlong toward the fountain, like lions from a thicket.
They crowd about their kinsman, who lies sleeping in the
basin's center.
They leap over the edge and begin to float in the basin,
licking their leader's snout and paws. The more they lick,
the darker
grows his threatening visage.
Finally he mingles with them,
springs abruptly to life, leaps down; and the entire
company
runs swiftly into the dark. The sky
hides its stars behind a cloud. Sober thinkers
call this
the abduction of the leader –
and, since the first drops are sparkling on the park bench,
they call this abduction of the leader a coming of rain.[1]
The rain slopes its yardsticks toward the earth,

building a net or a cage, high in the air, for a lion's family,
using neither knots nor nails.
There is a
drizzle of
warm rain.
No chill touches the throats of the shadows,
or the lion's throat.
You will be neither loved nor forgotten.
And, if you were a monster, a company of monsters
will resurrect you, at a late hour, out of the earth.
Rain and snow
will make known
your escape.
Not being subject to chest colds,
you will return to this world to spend the night.
For no loneliness is deeper than the memory of miracles.
Thus, former inmates return to their prisons,
and doves to the Ark.

December 1967

1. There is an untranslatable play on the expressions *pokhishcheniye
vozhdya* ('abduction of the leader') and *priblizheniye dozhdya* ('com-
ing of rain').

Almost an Elegy

In days gone by I too have waited out
cold rains near columns of the Stock Exchange.[1]
And I assumed that it was God's own gift.
It may be that I was not wrong in this.
I too was happy once. I lived in bond
of angels. And I fought against fierce monsters.
At the main entranceway I lay in wait,
like Jacob at his ladder, for a lovely
girl running down the stairs.
                              But all of this
has gone, vanished forever – wholly hidden.
And gazing out the window, having written
the word 'where', I don't add a question mark.
It is September now. An orchard stands
before me. Distant thunder stuffs my ears.
The ripened pears hang down in the thick leaves
like signs of maleness. And my ears now let
the roaring rain invade my drowsy mind[2] –
as skinflints let poor kin into their kitchens:
a sound that's less than music, though it's more
than noise.

Autumn 1968

---

1. The former St Petersburg Stock Exchange building (*birzha*) now houses the Central Museum of Naval History.
2. This line echoes a famous line from Derzhavin – *chevo v moi dremlyushchi togda ne vkhodit um?* ('What then does not enter my drowsy mind?') – which Pushkin uses as an epigraph for his poem 'Autumn'.

Verses in April

Once again this past winter
I did not go mad. As for winter itself –
one glances; it's gone. But I can divide
the din of ice cracking from the green
shroud of earth. So I'm sane.
I wish myself well
at the coming of spring;
blinded by the Fontanka,[1]
I break myself up into dozens of parts.
I run my flat hand
up and over my face. The snow-crust is settling
in my brain, as it does in the woods.

Having lived to the time of gray hairs,
I observe how a tug threads its way,
among ice floes, toward open sea.
                               For me
to forgive you in writing would be
just as harsh and unfair
as to charge you with wrong.
                        Please excuse me
for this lofty style:
though there's *no* end to our discontent,
there's an end to our winters.[2]
For the essence of change lies in this –
in the wrangling of Muses who swarm
at Mnemosyne's banquet.

April 1969

1. The Fontanka is one of the two major rivers in Leningrad, the other being the Neva. In April its surface would be 'blinding' because still covered with ice.

2. Cf. the opening lines of Shakespeare's *Richard III*:

Now is the winter of our discontent
Made glorious summer by this sun of York.

A Winter Evening in Yalta

He has a sear Levantine face, its pock-
marks hiding under sideburns. As he gropes
for cigarettes, his fingers in the pack,
a dull ring on his right hand suddenly
refracts at least two hundred watts; my eye's
frail crystal cannot tolerate the flash.
I blink, and then he says as he inhales
a mouthful of blue smoke, 'Excuse it, please.'

Crimean January. Winter comes
as though to romp along the Black Sea shore.
The snow loses its grip on the thin-tipped
and spiny-margined leaves of agave plants.
The restaurants are nearly empty now.[1]
Ichthyosaurs belch their black smoke and soil
the roadstead. Rotting laurel permeates
the air. 'And will you drink this vile stuff?' 'Yes.'

A smile and twilight, then, and a carafe.
A barman in the distance wrings his hands,
describing circles, like a porpoise pup
around a fish-filled felucca. Squareness
of windows. Yellow flowers in pots. And snow-
flakes tumbling past. I beg you, moment, stay!
It's not that you're particularly fair
but rather that you're unrepeatable.

January 1969

1. Yalta is a summer resort, not a winter resort, despite its relatively
mild climate. Thus in January its many restaurants would be 'nearly
empty'.

Part 4

Verses on the Death of T. S. Eliot[1]

I

He died at start of year, in January.
His front door flinched in frost by the streetlamp.
There was no time for nature to display
the splendors of her choreography.
Black windowpanes shrank mutely in the snow.
The cold's town-crier stood beneath the light.
At crossings puddles stiffened into ice.
He latched his door on the thin chain of years.

The days he leaves to us will not declare
a bankruptcy of Muses. Poetry
is orphaned, yet it breeds within the glass
of lonely days, each echoing each, that swim
to distance. It will splash against the eye,
sink into lymph, like some Aeolian nymph,
a narcissistic friend. But in the rhyme
of years the voice of poetry stands plain.

With neither grimace nor maliciousness
death chooses from its bulging catalogue
the poet, not his words, however strong,
but just – unfailingly – the poet's self.
It has no use for thickets or for fields
or seas in their high, bright magnificence.
Death is a prodigal, it piles
a horde of hearts upon a wisp of time.[2]

Used Christmas trees had flared in vacant lots,
and broken baubles had been broomed away.

Winged angels nested warmly on their shelves.
A Catholic,[3] he lived till Christmas Day.
But, as the sea, whose tide has climbed and roared,
slamming the seawall, draws its warring waves
down and away, so he, in haste, withdrew
from his own high and solemn victory.

It was not God, but only time, mere time
that called him. The young tribe of giant waves
will bear the burden of his flight until
it strikes the far edge of its flowering fringe,
to bid a slow farewell, breaking against
the limit of the earth. Exuberant
in strength, it laughs, a January gulf
in that dry land of days where we remain.

II

Where are you, Magi, you who read men's souls?
Come now and hold his halo high for him.
Two grieving figures gaze upon the ground.
They sing. How very similar their songs!
Are they then maidens? One cannot be sure:
pain and not passion has defined their sex.
One seems an Adam, turning half away,
but, judging by his flow of hair, an Eve ...

America, where he was born and raised,
and England, where he died – they both incline
their somber faces as they stand, bereft,
on either side of his enormous grave.
And ships of cloud swim slowly heavenward.

But each grave is the limit of the earth.

Apollo, fling your garland down.
Let it be this poet's crown,
pledge of immortality,
in a world where mortals be.

Forests here will not forget
voice of lyre and rush of feet.
Only what remains alive
will deserve their memories.

Hill and dale will honor him.
Aeolus will guard his fame.
Blades of grass his name will hold,
just as Horace[4] had foretold.

Thomas Stearns, don't dread the sheep,
or the reaper's deadly sweep.
If you're not recalled by stone,
puffball drift will make you known.

Thus it is that love takes flight.
Once for all. Into the night.
Cutting through all words and cries,
seen no more, and yet alive.

You have gone where others are.
We, in envy of your star,
call that vast and hidden room,
thoughtlessly, 'the realm of gloom'.

Wood and field will not forget.
All that lives will know you yet –

as the body holds in mind
lost caress of lips and arms.

12 January 1965

1. Brodsky was in exile in the Soviet Far North when Eliot died on
4 January 1965, and did not learn of Eliot's death until a week later.
He completed this poem within twenty-four hours of receiving the
news. The literary model for the poem is, of course, W. H. Auden's
'In Memory of W. B. Yeats (d. Jan. 1939)'.

2. Since the Russian words *smert* ('death') and *poeziya* ('poetry') are
both feminine in gender and are referred to by the same pronoun,
ona (literally, 'she'), the connection between death and poetry in the
second and third stanzas is clearer and more explicit in the original
than it can be made in translation.

3. Eliot was an Anglican Catholic; it would be natural for a Russian
poet to refer to him, as Brodsky does, simply as *katolik* ('a Catholic').

4. The reference is to Horace's ode *Exegi monumentum aere peren-
nius* ('I have raised a monument more lasting than bronze') (Book III,
Ode 30). The first two words appear as the epigraph to a celebrated
poem by Pushkin; it is in Pushkin's poem rather than Horace's that
the 'blades of grass' are said to preserve the poet's memory: the feet
of pilgrims visiting the poet's grave wear a path through the sur-
rounding grass.

To a Certain Poetess

I have a touch of normal classicism
and you, my dear, a bad case of sarcasm.
A woman whose career involves sales taxes
is apt to let caprice govern her life.
You've seen an 'iron age' in our present epoch.
But I had never dreamed (to change the topic)
that I, whose soberness of style was classic,
would balance on the thin edge of a knife.

It seems that death-of-friendship now has struck us.
This is the start of an extended ruckus.
Yet you can blame no one except old Bacchus
if you should lack advancement where you toil.
I am the same now, leaving this arena,
as when I entered it. Yet I stand in a
shroud of volcanic ash, like Herculaneum,
and cannot lift a hand to save your soul.

So let us call it quits. I've lost my freedom.
I eat potatoes; I sleep in a hay-barn.
On this thief's head, I may report, no hat's worn:
my bright bald-spot betrays a thinning trend.
I am a parrot, a mere imitator.
You've put this parrot-life safely away, dear.
And when the Law pitchforked me out of favor
your dire prognosis cheered me up no end.

There is one thing forbidden by the Muses
to those who serve them.[1] Yet the Muses' service
renders a poet's hands divinely nervous.

None then can doubt God's presence or His power.
One 'poet' sits preparing memoranda.
Another sighs, muffling a murmur. And a
third, following a well-rehearsed agenda,
plucks lines from other poets like spring flowers.

Death surely will make plain that mere sarcasm
can't keep up with life's energy. Its prism
can only magnify life's cytoplasm.
Alas, it can't illuminate life's core.
Thus, bound in long-term service to the Muse, I
prefer the classic to the mere sarcastic,
although I, like the Syracusan mystic,[2]
might view the world from a deep barrel's floor.

Let's call it quits. A sign, no doubt, of flabbiness.
Foreseeing your sarcastic lack of sadness,
in this remote place, I would bless non-drabness:
the buzzing of a blindingly bright wasp
above a simple daisy can unnerve me.
I see the sheer abyss that lies before me.
My consciousness whirls like a spinning fanwheel
about the steady axis of my past.

The shoemaker builds boots. The busy baker
produces pretzels. And the necromancer
leafs through huge folio-volumes. So the sinner
makes special efforts, sinning every day.
Sleek dolphins tow a tripod through the billows.
Those things that seemed most real to old Apollo's
calm glance will prove, at last, most hollow.
The forests roar, and the high heavens are deaf.

The Fall will soon be with us. In briefcases
school notebooks find their nest. And enchantresses

like you with care pile up their braided tresses
into a shield against the wind's cold breath.
I recollect our trip to the Crimea,
when both of us loved nature, loved to see a
wild landscape – the more beautiful the freer.
I am astonished, madam, and I grieve.

September 1965

1. An allusion to Pushkin's aphoristic line: '*Sluzheniye muz ne terpit suyety*' ('The Muses' service brooks no vanity').
2. The reference is to Diogenes the Cynic, who is reported by Seneca to have lived in a tub.

A Letter in a Bottle

Forward, it seems, is where mouth and nose[1]
point, or where any façade is turned.
Backward would be the reverse of those.
'Forward' and 'backward' are shifting terms.
But since the bow[1] of my ship points North,
the gaze of the passenger seeks the West
(and thus he is staring straight overboard);
switching his place makes it more complex.
Physicists have devised vectors which
plot a ship's course when it's under full sail.
Ships strung on vectors may roll and pitch.
Vectors are bodyless, like the soul.

Joyous Leviathans slap their tails,
swimming head downward beneath the waves.
Gossamer vectors of harpoon-nails
hammer out doom on their careless days.
From towering crags the fair siren horde
lift their strong voices in unison
while stalwart Ulysses, alone, on board,
is cleaning his pistol, a Smith-Wesson.
A people that's fixing the frontier fast
between Good and Evil should recognize:
a man who appears to delve into the past
in fact may move forward before its eyes.
Under a canopy, stretched full length,
sleeping in warmth (gauged in centigrade),
one to whom cesium[2] lends heel-strength
kicks at the star-cover overhead.
That bard[3] who tried vainly to heal the sea

with music and alum and iodine,
chasing a trope to antiquity,
surely would now take a modern line.

Janus, your faces that stare both ways,
one facing lifeward, and one toward death,
give the whole world a full circle shape,
though we may dive to its farthest depth.
If at right angles you blindly sail,
you'll run into passion, like Sweden's shore.
And if you spin between Good and Ill
you'll end in Leviathan's giant maw.
I – like a knight who rides proudly forth
and lays down his life, while he saves his steed –
have voyaged with honor, my course: due North.
Where did I end? That you must decide.
Remember, I beg you, though spirits soar,
sails are no substitute for real wings.
Long before Newton, old Shakespeare saw
this basic sameness in both strivings.

I sailed with honor, but my frail craft
wounded its side on a jagged reef.
I wet my fingers; the Finnish Gulf
suddenly proved to be very deep.
Hiding my grief, I now shielded my eyes
under my hand, but my gaze could not reach –
although I applied my binoculars –
as far as the sand of the youth-camp beach.
Snow was now falling; I'd run aground
on the dark reef, my port side was high –
like the *Admiral Apraksin*[4] of naval renown –
though not by what she was stranded by.

Icebergs are silently swimming South.
My colors flutter against the gale.
Mice scurry noiselessly toward the prow.
Gurgling, the sea washes through my hull.
My heart is pounding; the whirling snow
muffles till springtime the mailcoach blast,
dropping the horn's pitch from *la* to *do*,
hiding the crow's nest from my tired glance.
The stern melts away, but the snowdrifts grow.
Ice chandeliers hang as though from trees.
The view's panoramic, the heavens show
three hundred sixty, and more, degrees.
The stars are aflame and the ice agleam.
My ship as it rolls makes a jangling noise.
The figurehead's eyes pour out lachrymose streams –
eyes which have counted a billion waves.

My teeth are now chattering in Morse code
with wires for Marconi and Prof. Popóv,
inventors of wireless; for them I load
my carrier-pigeons and wave them off.
Space flows, like beer, through my beard and mouth.
Let Lindbergh stay where the Zeppelins are,
in the huge hangar. I've had enough
of ragged black crow-wings that sing 'caw-caw'.
I've lost all count of both days and clouds.
The lens of my eye has no faith in gleams.
When lights seem to beckon, my mind, like a guard,
whispers in warning: 'It's just a dream.'
Adieu, Thomas Alva, who spoiled the night.
Adieu, Archimedes and Faraday.
As leaky three-masters resist the sea's weight,
my small candles keep the huge dark at bay.
(Today, it may be, for the final time

I'll wage war at cards with the stableman.
And you'll mark the score once again with the pen
that once I had used to write love poems.)

My ship's side is broken. The Gulf is broad.
No one is guilty. Our pilot is God.
He is the one Person we address.
The will to salvation breeds humbleness.
Against you, St Francis, o holy man,
I enter a mournful complaint; but then,
inspecting this gaping hole, I am sure
it is my ship's stigma, and I am pure.
The tide, it appears, has begun to rise,
revealing a simple but vital truth:
what's sweet in the land of the olive trees
can cause bitter pain in the frozen north.
One doesn't need field-glasses made by Zeiss
to see this plain fact: I have lost my case
more quickly than pagans who sue to lie
with mistresses false or unwilling wives.
I see that the water is now chest-deep.
And I must bed down for my final sleep.
Since no one is coming to say good-bye,
I'll shake several hands now, definitively.

Dear Dr Freud, I will say good-bye
to you who have managed, intuitively
(yet somehow outside us), to throw a span
across the soul's river from groin to brain.
Adieu to the prophet who said, 'Forsooth,
you've nothing to lose but your chains.' In truth
there's conscience as well – if it comes to that.
So much for your truth, I say, Karl, old chap.
And you, whose beard also was something to see,

Count Leo Tolstoy, your high Excellency,
who loved to tread grass with your bony feet,
you too I must leave now. You too were right.
Adieu, Albert Einstein, most learned man,
I've not yet inspected what your mind spanned,
but I've built a hut in the space-time whole:
time is a wave and curved space – a whale.

Nature itself was a dream I dreamed.
The sleuths of its bounties, who merely seemed:
Newton and Kepler and Robert Boyle[5]
(Kepler who made the moon tell its tale) –
these were all figures within my mind:
Mendel with specimens, Darwin with finds
(bones of macaco), and Winter and Spring,
May, August, all my friends to whom I cling.
I dreamed the hot and I dreamed the cold;
I dreamed a square and I dreamed a globe.
The grass's small rustling, a tit-mouse song.
And often I dreamed that I must be wrong.
I dreamed the dense dark and the glow of waves.
And sometimes in dreams I would see my own face.
I dreamed I was hearing a horse's neigh.
But death is a mirror that does not lie.
When I die, or more accurately, awake,
if it's boring *there* in the first few days,
then, o my dream-visions, I'll give to you
the gratitude that will be your due.
But note: the mere fact that I make such boasts
is a sign that I want to preserve old ghosts,
a sign that I still am a bit in love,
a sign that my sleep is as deep as the cave.

And so, in returning my tongue and eye

to the whitecaps of seventy lines gone by
(to make the connection with shepherds' crooks),[6]
I'm taking my station again on deck.
All that I see now is my ship's bow.
The figurehead's mouth is concealed by snow.
Her delicate breast is a white snowbank.
This frail floating coffin will soon be sunk.
As I head for the bottom, there to remain,
I'd like to have one matter perfectly plain
(since I'll not travel a homeward line):
where are you taking me, vector mine?

I'd like to think there was sense in my song,
that what I had formerly called 'the dawn'
will break in the future, as once it did,
a gloss on life's vanishing calendar-pad.
I'd like to think, or at least to dream,
that children will laugh as they play ball games
or build their small houses of wooden blocks.
I'd like to believe (in the face of shocks)
that life will send divers where I've down-swirled,
directing them straight to the 'other world'.

It's shameful, my weakness! But I dare hope,
dear friends, that a merciful God will keep
intact for a moment those things that I
had no time to see with my own two eyes:
Crimea, the Caucasus, deathless Rome,
the Alps, the Euphrates, America's span;
Torzhok,[7] where the cleaning of boots is a rite;
a series of virtues in blinding light,
though I would not venture to write them down.
You could thus celebrate, one by one,
Duty and Honor and Thriftiness

(although I'm not certain that you exist).
I also hope that a certain Swede[8]
will save the whole world from atomic dread,
that man-yellow tigers[9] will mute their roar,
that up-to-date Newtons will crunch Eve's core
and sprinkle the woods with the apple's pips,
that saucers[10] will grace the celestial cups.

Adieu, then, and let the wind howl its fill.
There is no cause to condemn its blast.
The Future may grieve over present ill;
however you twist it, it's not the Past.
Let Kant blow his whistle as he stands guard.
And let Feuerbach[11] in old Weimar pipe:
'The flip of a switch simply can't cut short
the pulsating stream of our inner life.'
Perhaps he is right. And perhaps he's not.
In any case (now that the wind has died)
I know for a fact that the stream will stop
as soon as the Old Woman puts out the light.
May life then persist and the great horn bray
at sight of a snail in a hollow tree,
while I in my modest and halting way
set sail, in the words of old Rabelais,
for the shadowy shores of the 'Great Maybe'.[12]
        (washed out)
You'll pardon, dear madam, my heart's blurred flame;
you know the high haven at which I aimed.
You know that I left my ship's compass unread,
making visual contact with *you* instead.

I dream of an avenue filled with dogs,
park benches, bright blooms in a flower-box.
With nosegays of violets at your pale throat,

you are, my dear madam, superbly coiffed.

Now when I lower my somber gaze,
I see a white headland – your jersey blouse,
and feet that are shod in petite lifeboats:
each, like a jib, boasts a tiny bow.

Above them I see (o celestial harps!) –
like a sailor's wide collar – your white-striped scarf,
and tumbling brown waves that can't be kept down,
in which I should greatly prefer to drown.

Two eyebrows like wings of delightful birds,
spanning a gaze that's too vast for worlds,
that knows no frontiers, either future or past,
but makes the Invisible show its Face.

Madam, if heart is conjoined to glance
(shining, and broken, and held askance),
I gladly note that in your own case
no bar obtrudes between heart and gaze.

This is more, madam, than heaven's light,
since at the Pole one can crawl about
hundreds of years and not see a star –
life's an absorber of light and air.

Madam, your heart – or rather your gaze
(like delicate fingers that give things shape) –
generates feelings and lends them form
by means of its own internal warmth.
        (washed out)
And in this bottle that lies at your feet,
a shy, orphaned witness of my defeat,

you seek, like an astronaut far out in space,
for life that has already ceased to exist.
The neck of the bottle contains pure grief.
The label will bring you back to yourself
(you'll know it by heart once you've read it through).
The bottom is where I'll be waiting for you.

In order, dear madam, to banish spleen
we'll cry, 'Bottoms up!' – in the words of Flynn.
As in that old movie, 'Against all Flags',
the whole world's reflected in curved green glass.
          (washed out)
Remember me, madam, whenever the sea
comes hurrying toward you in crashing spray;
remember me, madam, when verses pound,
remember me, madam, when words resound.

The sea, my dear madam, is someone's talk.
I'm deaf and my stomach is past all hope.
I've now drunk my fill and I'm choked with speech.
          (washed out)
Remember me, madam, whenever the sea . . .
          (washed out)
What couplets may bring me I must pay back
in days or in hours on my lonely track –
for instance, these days in the snowy waste.
It's death alone, madam, that can't be repaid.
          (washed out)
What did the sorrowful bullfinch chirp
to the cat that had climbed to the poor bird's perch?
He said, without shifting his eyes from his foe's,
'I thought that you never would come. Alas!'

1965

114

1. The Russian word *nos* means both 'nose' and 'bow' (of a ship).
2. Cesium is used in Soviet rocket fuel.
3. The reference is to Orpheus and also to Arion.
4. The Russian cruiser *Admiral Apraksin* – named for Count F. M. Apraksin (1661–1728), chief of the Admiralty under Peter the Great – ran aground in the Gulf of Finland in 1900. Professor Alexander S. Popov (1859–1906), who had developed wireless telegraphy at about the same time as Marconi (1895–6), established radio communication with the disabled vessel from a point some thirty miles distant.
5. The original has 'Boyle-Mariotte' rather than 'Robert Boyle'. In Russia the law of gases – which Anglo-Americans call 'Boyle's law' and Frenchmen 'Mariotte's law' – is called 'the law of Boyle-Mariotte' (*Boilya-Mariotta zakon*). Brodsky is making a playful reference to the common blunder among Russian schoolboys, who take 'Boyle-Mariotte' as a single hyphenated name.
6. The Russian word for 'whitecap' is *barashka*, literally, 'lamb'; hence the 'connection' with shepherds, which is lost in English. Brodsky is also alluding to Rabelais' punning phrase: *Revenons à nos moutons*. (The word *barashka* does not actually occur in the earlier passage.)
7. A Russian town located on the main road between Leningrad and Moscow; here a symbol for the remote provinces. Since many of Torzhok's streets are unpaved, thus either dusty or muddy, there are more dirty boots among its inhabitants than people to clean them; hence the 'cleaning of boots' is a 'rite'.
8. This is a reference to Dag Hammarskjöld (1905–61), secretary-general of the United Nations from 1953 until his death.
9. Literally, 'yellow tigers', i.e., the Chinese Communists.
10. The reference is to 'flying saucers' (unidentified flying objects).
11. The allusion to Feuerbach is ironical; Brodsky is well aware that Feuerbach was a materialist and reductionist, who denied any form of life after death.
12. In response to Cardinal Châtillon's inquiry about his health, the dying Rabelais wrote: '. . . je vais quérir un grand peut-être.'

Einem alten Architekten in Rom[1]

I

Let's take a carriage – if indeed a shade
can really ride upon a carriage-seat
(especially on such a rainy day),
and if a shade can tolerate the jolting,
and if the horse does not tear off the harness –
then we will find a topless carriage, spread
umbrellas, climb aboard, and clatter off,
wordless among the squares of Königsberg.

II

Rain nibbles at the leaves, stones, hems of waves.
The river licks its chops and mutters darkly;
its fish look down from the bridge railings, stunned
sheer out of time, into eternity,
as though thrown up by an exploding wave.
(The rising tide itself has left no mark.)
A carp gleams in its coat of steel chain-mail.
The trees are vaguely whispering in German.

III

Hand up your Zeiss field-glasses to the cabby.
Let him turn off and leave the trolley tracks.
Does he not hear the clanging bell behind us?
A streetcar hurries on its millionth run.
Its bell bangs loudly as it passes us,
drowning the clip-clop beat of horses' hooves.
High ruins on the hills bend down and peer
into the mirror of the streetcar's windows.

IV

The leaves of grass are trembling timidly.
Acanthi, nimbi, doves (both male and female),
atlantes, cupids, lions, nymphs, all hide
their stumps behind their backs, plainly embarrassed.
Narcissus could not hope to find a pool
more clear than that retreating streetcar window,
behind which passengers have formed a wall,
risking amalgamation for a moment.

V

Twilight of early morning. River mist.
The windswept butts of cigarettes are circling
the trash bin. A young archeologist
pours shards into the hood of his striped parka.
It's drizzling. In the midst of vacant lots,
among vast ruined buildings powdered over
with broken stone, astonished, you behold
a modest bust of Field Marshal Suvorov.[2]

VI

The noisy banquet of the bombing planes
is still. March rain scrubs soot-flakes from the portals.
Rudders of wrecked planes jut up here and there.
Tall plumes of broken walls now seem immortal.
And if one were to dig here – I would guess –
these battered homes, like haylofts under needles,
would give good grounds for finding happiness
beneath a quaternary shroud of fragments.

VII

A maple tree flaunts its first sticky leaves.
Power saws are whining in the Gothic church.
Rooks[3] cough in the deserted city playground.

Park benches gleam with rain. A nanny-goat
behind a fence stares at that distant spot
where the first green has spread across the farmyard.

VIII

Spring peers through empty windows at herself,
and knows herself in instant recognition.
The tides of war reveal to human sight
what hitherto was hidden from man's vision.
Life rages from both sides of broken walls,
though lacking trait of stone or face of granite.
It looks ahead, since there's no wall behind . . .
Although the bushes are alive with shadows.

IX

But if you are no apparition, if
you are living flesh, then take a note from nature.
And, having made a sketch of this terrain,
find for your soul a wholly different structure.
Throw out dull bricks, throw out cement and stone,
battered to dust – by what? – a winged propeller.
And lend the soul that open, airy look
remembered from your classroom's model atom.

X

And let an empty space begin to gape
among your feelings. After languorous sorrow
let fear explode, followed by cresting rage.
It's possible in this atomic epoch,
when cliffs tremble like reeds, for us to save
both hearts and walls – if we will reinforce them
with that same power that now portends their death.
I trembled when I heard the words, 'My darling'.

XI

You may compare, or weigh in the mind's eye,
true love, and passion, and the listlessness
that follows pain. An astronaut who streaks
toward Mars longs suddenly to walk on earth.
But a caress remote from loving arms,
when miles take you aback, stabs at your brain
harder than kisses: separation's sky
is solider than any ceilinged shelter.

XII

Cheep, cheep-chireep. Cheep-cheep. You look above
and out of sorrow or, it may be, habit
you glimpse a Königsberg among the twigs.
And why shouldn't a bird be called a Königs-
berg, a Caucasus, a Rome? – When all
around us there are only bricks and broken
stones; no objects, only words. And yet –
no lips. The only sound we hear is twittering.

XIII

You will forgive my words their clumsiness.
That starling, finding them a provocation,
draws even with me: *cheep, ich liebe dich,*
and then leaves me behind: *cheep-cheep, ich sterbe.*
Put sketchbook and binoculars away
and turn your dry back on the weathercock.
Close your umbrella, as a rook would close
its wings. Its handle-tail reveals the capon.

XIV

The harness traces stand in shreds ... Where is
the horse? ... The clatter of his hooves has died ...
The carriage rolls among the empty hills,

looping through ruins, coasting fast. Two long
breech-straps trail out behind it ... There are wheel-tracks
in the sand. The bushes buzz with ambushes ...

The sea, whose crests repeat the silhouettes
of landscapes that the wheels have left behind them,
draws in its billows to the land's frontier,
spreading them like the news – like the Good News –
and thus destroys the likeness of the waves
and hills, caressing the wet carriage-spokes.

1964

1. The title is modelled on Wallace Stevens' *To an Old Philosopher
in Rome*. The Stevens poem, which is about the dignity of a man
approaching death – 'a kind of total grandeur at the end' – is dedi-
cated to an 'old philosopher' (George Santayana); Brodsky's poem,
which is about the devastation of a city, is dedicated, with a touch of
irony, to an 'old architect'. When Brodsky visited Königsberg (now
Kaliningrad) in 1962 he found the city – seventeen years after the war
– still largely in ruins and unreconstructed.

2. Count A. V. Suvorov (1730–1800) was commander of the
Russian armies under Catherine the Great. In the late 1940s the Soviet
authorities placed a small statue of Suvorov on a large pedestal near
the palace of the Elector (*Kurfürst*) of Königsberg which had previ-
ously held a large statue of the Elector himself.

3. In Russia the rook (*grach*) is considered a symbol of springtime.

Two Hours in an Empty Tank

'Demon, I am bored...'
  Pushkin[1]

I

I am an anti-fascist anti-Faust.
Ich liebe life, but chaos I adore.
Ich bin prepared, genosse offizieren,
dem zeit zum Faust quite briefly to spazieren.[2]

II

In old Krakow he mourned his vaterland,
not being swayed by Polish propaganda,
and sought the bright stone of philosophers,
doubting the depth of his abilities.
He snatched up handkerchiefs that women dropped.
He warmed to questions of sexology.
He starred on the department's polo team.

He studied the card-player's catechism
and crunched the candy of Cartesianism.
And then he crawled down the artesian well
of ego-centrism. But Klausewitz's
sly craft of soldiering remained somehow
beyond his ken – perhaps because his own
dear vater's craft was cabinet-making.

Zum beispiel, cholera, glaucoma, plague,
und auch tuberculosis, roared and raged.
He tried to save himself by puffing schwarze
cigaretten. Moors and gypsies drew him.
He was anointed Bachelor of Arts,

then won his laurels as Licentiate,
and sang in seminar of dinosaurs.

The man was German: German was his mind.
And what is more, *cogito ergo sum.*
And über alles Germany, of course.
(Well-known Vienna waltzes fill the ear.)
He left Krakow without shedding a tear
and in his *drozhky* quickly drove away
to take his Chair and lift a stein of beer.

III

A new moon glimmers in the ragged clouds.
A man stoops over a huge folio volume.
A crease deepens between his bushy brows.
His eyes show demon glints of arabesque.
His trembling fingers hold a soft lead pencil.
The Arab delegate, Meph-ibn-Stophel,
peers from a corner at the Faustian profile.

Candles flare up. Beneath a chest a mouse
makes scratching sounds. 'Herr doktor, it's midnight.'
'Jawohl, muss schlafen, schlafen.' Two black mouths
say 'Meow.' A jüdisch frau slips silently
from the dark kitchen with an omelet
that sizzles in salt-pork. The herr doktor
writes on an envelope: 'Gott strafe England, London,
        Francis Bacon.'

Enter and *exeunt*: devils and thoughts.
Enter and *exeunt*: seasons and guests.
The costume-changes, weather-changes, change
of words, can't be kept track of. Thus the years
roll by unnoticed. He knew Arabic,
not Sanskrit. Late, alas, in life he found

his eine kleine fräulein, Margareta.

Faust sent an urgent message off to Cairo:
consigned his soul *pro forma* to the devil.
Meph came non-stoph; then Faust put on a new
costume, and, glancing in the glass, convinced
himself that he had been made young at last,
to last forever. He visited, with flowers,
her virgin room. Und *veni, vidi, vici.*

IV

Ich liebe clearness. Ja. Ich liebe neatness.
Ich bin to beg you not to call it weakness.
Do you sugchest dat he lufft flower-girlss?
Ich untershtant dat das ist ganze urchent.
But this arrangement macht der grosse minus.
Die teutschne sprache,[3] macht der grosse cosine:
and nein, one's heart can't be consumed at home.

It's silly to expect alles from men:
'Oh, moment, stay, thou art so very fair.'
The devil walks among us hour by hour
and waits, each moment, for this fatal phrase.
But men, mein liebe herren, insofar
as they're unsure about their stronger feelings,
will lie like troopers, conscientiously,
but Goethe-like, they'll let no chance slip by.

Und grosser dichter Goethe tripped and fell,
which makes his theme ganz problematical.
And Thomas Mann spoiled his subscription list,[4]
while *cher* Gounod embarrassed his *artiste.*[5]
For art is art is art ... A heavenly song
is more befitting than hitting the wrong

note in recital. Kunst needs feeling's truth.

Faust may, in the end, have been afraid to die.
He knew exactly where the devils lie.
He had devoured the works of Avicenna
and Galen. He knew how to dry das was-
ser on the knee, and gauge tree-age from cross-
sections. Could he track distant stars? He could.

But Dr Faust knew less than nichts of God.

v
There is a mystic lore; faith; and the Lord.
They differ and yet have some points in common.
The flesh saved some men; others it destroyed.
Men who lack faith are both blind and inhuman.

God, then, looks down. And men look up. But each
has a peculiar interest of his own.
While God's being is natural, mere man
has limitations which, I trust, are plain.

Man has a ceiling of his own, although
its place and shape are not clearly defined.
The flatterer finds a corner in men's hearts;[6]
men see the devil, but to life they're blind.

Such then was Dr Faust. And such again
were Marlowe, Goethe, Thomas Mann – alas –
the milling mob of bards and thinking men
und readers drawn from a quite different class.

Time's torrent sweeps away their half-baked schemes,
their – donnerwetter! – test-tubes, their last traces.
And may God grant them all the time they need
to ask, 'Where to?' and heed the shouting Muses.

An honest German won't wait to discover
der weg zurück, even when he is invited.
He takes his Walter[7] from his heavy trousers
and goes for good into the Walter-Klosett.

VI

Fräulein, pray tell, was ist das inkubus?
Inkubus, das ist eine kleine globus.
Noch grosser dichter Goethe framed a rebus.
Und, hocus-pocus, vicious heron flocks
rose from the fog of Weimar to purloin
the key from his deep pocket. Eckermann's
sharp eye was not enough to save us then.
And now, matrosen, we are on the rocks.

Some tasks are truly our own spirit's tasks.
All mystic lore's an unsuccessful mask
for our attempts to deal with them. To ask
the sense of ich bin, otherwise, is mad.
Zum beispiel, ceiling: prolegomenon
to roof. What, *qua* poet, he gains; *qua* man,
he loses.[8] I recall the Virgin, stand-
ing in a niche, and breakfast served in bed.

September's here again. The moon is full.
I'm bored. Against my legs a gray witch purrs.
I've tucked a hatchet underneath my pil-
low... If we had some schnapps... so... abgemacht!
Jawohl. September. Dispositions sour.
On the mud field a skidding tractor roars.
Ich liebe life and the *Völkisch Beobachter*.
Gut nacht, mein liebe herren. Ja, gut nacht.

September 1965

1. The epigraph is from Pushkin's poem, *A Scene from Faust*.

2. The 'German' in this poem reproduces the fractured and ungrammatical speech of Soviet soldiers who served in Germany during the Second World War, spiced by an occasional Yiddish expression. In the original text the scattered 'German' words and phrases are printed in the Cyrillic (Russian) alphabet, which makes them seem even more grotesque. In this translation they are left unitalicized in an attempt to produce something like the effect of the original.

3. An old form of the expression *die deutsche Sprache* ('the German language').

4. Mann 'spoiled his subscription list' by publishing *Dr Faustus*, a work so disappointing (in Brodsky's view) that it caused many readers who had signed up for Mann's complete works (in Russian translation) to cancel their subscriptions.

5. Gounod 'embarrassed' the singer who had to take the part of Margareta in his opera *Faust*; she would have preferred a better role.

6. This line is a slight variation on a line in Krylov's fable, *The Raven and the Fox*: *I v serdtse lstets vsegda otyshchet ugolok* ('And the flatterer always finds a corner in the heart').

7. The Walter is a kind of German pistol, something like the Luger.

8. The Russian phrase *poemoi bolshe, chelovekom – nitsshe* contains a neologizing pun. The word *nitsshe* is formed by adding the Russian comparative ending – *she* to the Polish word *nić* ('nothing'); it is also a Russian form of the name 'Nietzsche'.

From *The School Anthology:*
Albert Frolov[1]

Albert Frolov loved silence as a boy.
His mother was a postal clerk, whose portion
was rubber stamps. As for Albert's old man,
he died to save the Finn's autonomy,[2]
having secured timely perpetuation
of the family name, but not knowing his son.

Young Albert nursed his talents quietly.
I still recall the large bumps on his temple:
he fainted in zoology, and fell,
crashing, beneath his desk, unsinewed by
the sight of his dissected frog, example –
as he had failed to prove – of life *sans* soul.

The sweep of Albert's thought took him as far
as engineering school, where he was summoned
by archangelic powers to mortal fray.
Then, like a sinning cherub, he dropped down
to earth from his high cloud, and found a trumpet
ready to hand, calling for him to play.

Silence can be prolonged in shape of sound,
like the unrolling of a narrow ribbon.
Playing a trumpet solo, he observed
with squinting eyes the bell-mouth of his horn
where fireflies glowed, ignited by the stage lights,
until applause welled up and snuffed them out.

Such were his nights. But what about his days?
By day the stars cannot be seen. Not even

from bottoms of deep wells. His wife resigned,
without washing his socks. His mother stayed
and tried to care for him. He started drinking,
then took to drugs – whatever he could find.

– No doubt from misery, or blank despair.
Unhappily, I lack firm information.
The drugs, it seems, produce a new time-span.
When playing, you can 'see' ahead eight bars;
with use of certain drugs this span is doubled.
In 'Palaces of Culture', where his band

performed, the mirrors on the walls took in,
politely and yet somberly, those features
which eczema had stamped with scars and pits.
They charged him with corrupting his whole team
and, tired of trying to 're-educate' him,
they fired him. Through tight lips he muttered, 'Shit!'

Then, like a fading *A*, having derived
no clear conclusions from his daily hassle
that would bring gleams to any idle eye –
he marched across the margin of his life,
made absolute the concept of dismissal,
and disappeared, leaving no trace behind.

On January second, late at night,
my steamer eased into the dock at Sochi.
Wanting a drink, I strolled at random through
the narrow streets that led up to the lights
of the great city from the darkened dockside,
and came upon the Cascade Restaurant.

It was the New Year holiday. Palm boughs
were festooned with resplendent fake pine needles.
A swarm of tipsy Georgians circled past
my table, singing 'Tbiliso'.[3] The pulse
of life throbs everywhere; in this place also.
I'd heard the solo, now I raised my face

above the bottles. The Cascade was full.
Trying to reach the stage, through a sheer bedlam
of sounds and smells, I glimpsed a stooped, thin back.
I touched a sleeve, and then I shouted 'Al!'
A ghastly, monstrous mask turned slowly toward me,
covered with swollen sores and brittle scabs.

His stringy hair, untouched by scabs or sores,
his eyes – were all that now remained to witness
the schoolboy of a dozen years ago.
Was this the lad who'd thrown those furtive stares
– as I in turn had done, I must confess it –
across his desk at my poor scribbled notes?

'What brings you here in the off-season?' Skin
as dry and wrinkled as the bark of trees is.
Eyes that were like twin squirrels peeping out
of hollows. 'How are things with you?' 'O, I'm
a Jason hibernating here in Colchis.
My eczema calls for a warmer climate.'

We went out then. The streetlights, widely spaced,
prevented the full merging of the heavens
with avenues. The policeman was an Ossete.
My escort, even here, clutching his case[4]
and keeping to the shadows, pressed the question:
'Are you alone here?' 'Yes, I am – I think.'

Was he a Jason? Hardly. A Job, then,
refusing to blame Heaven, simply blending
into the night – matter of life and death.
A strip of shore, the rustle of unseen
palm trees, and from the East the pungent odor
of wet seaweed – then suddenly a lurch,

and from the dock a momentary flash.
A sound began to move, threading the silence,
swimming to catch our ship's fast-moving stern.

And I could hear the strains of his sad song:
'How high the moon, how very high the moon!'

1969

1. *The School Anthology* is a projected cycle of forty poems, each of which is devoted to one of Brodsky's grammar-school classmates. Fifteen of the poems have been completed, but only five have thus far been published (in Russian).

2. An ironic reference to the official Soviet claim that the 1939–40 invasion of Finland was an act of 'liberation'.

3. The Georgian title means 'O, Tbilisi [Tiflis]'.

4. In Russian: *chelovek s futlyarom* ('a man with a case') – an allusion to Chekhov's short story *Chelovek v futlyare* ('A Man in a Case').

A Halt in the Desert[1]

So few Greeks live in Leningrad today
that we have razed a Greek church, to make space
for a new concert hall, built in today's
grim and unhappy style. And yet a con-
cert hall with more than fifteen hundred seats[2]
is not so grim a thing. And who's to blame
if virtuosity has more appeal
than the worn banners of an ancient faith?
Still, it is sad that from this distance now
we see, not the familiar onion domes,
but a grotesquely flattened silhouette.
Yet men are not so heavily in debt
to the grim ugliness of balanced forms
as to the balanced forms of ugliness.

I well remember how the church succumbed.
I was then making frequent springtime calls
at the home of a Tartar family
who lived nearby. From their front window one
could clearly see the outline of the church.
It started in the midst of Tartar talk,
but soon the racket forced its rumbling way
into our conversation, mingling with,
then drowning out, our steady human speech.
A huge power shovel clanked up to the church,
an iron ball dangling from its boom, and soon
the walls began to give way peaceably.
Not to give way would be ridiculous
for a mere wall in face of such a foe.
Moreover, the power shovel may have thought

the wall a dead and soulless thing and thus,
to a degree, like its own self. And in
the universe of dead and soulless things
resistance is regarded as bad form.
Next came the dump trucks, then the bulldozers . . .
So, in the end, I sat – late that same night –
among fresh ruins in the church's apse.
Night yawned behind the altar's gaping holes.
And through these open altar wounds I watched
retreating streetcars as they slowly swam
past phalanxes of deathly pale streetlamps.
I saw now through the prism of that church
a swarm of things that churches do not show.

Some day, when we who now live are no more,
or rather after we have been, there will
spring up in what was once our space
a thing of such a kind as will bring fear,
a panic fear, to those who knew us best.
But those who knew us will be very few.
The dogs, moved by old memory, still lift
their hindlegs at a once familiar spot.
The church's walls have long since been torn down,
but these dogs see the church walls in their dreams –
dog-dreams have cancelled out reality.
Perhaps the earth still holds that ancient smell:
asphalt can't cover up what a dog sniffs.
What can this building be to such as dogs!
For them the church still stands; they see it plain.
And what to people is a patent fact
leaves them entirely cold. This quality
is sometimes called 'a dog's fidelity'.
And, if I were to speak in earnest of
the 'relay race of human history',

I'd swear by nothing but this relay race –
this race of all the generations who
have sniffed, and who will sniff, the ancient smells.

So few Greeks live in Leningrad today,
outside of Greece, in general, so few –
too few to save the buildings of the faith.
And to have faith in buildings – none asks that.
It is one thing to bring a folk to Christ;
to bear His cross is something else again.[3]
Their duty was a single thing and clear,
but they lacked strength to live that duty whole.
Their unploughed fields grew thick with vagrant weeds.
'Thou who doest sow, keep thy sharp plough at hand
and we shall tell thee when thy grain is ripe.'
They failed to keep their sharp ploughs close at hand.

Tonight I stare out through the black window
and think about that point to which we've come,
and then I ask myself: from which are we
now more remote – the world of ancient Greece,
or Orthodoxy? Which is closer now?
What lies ahead? Does a new epoch wait
for us? And, if it does, what duty do we owe? –
What sacrifices must we make for it?

1966

1. During the mid-1960s a Greek Orthodox church was torn down and a large steel-and-glass structure – the 'October' Concert Hall – erected in its place in a section of Leningrad not far from where Brodsky then lived.

2. Literally, 'over a thousand seats'; in fact, the October Concert Hall seats more than four thousand.

3. An untranslatable play on words: *natsiyu krestit*, literally, 'to baptize a nation', and *krest nesti*, literally, 'to bear a cross'.

Adieu, Mademoiselle Véronique

I

If I end my days in the shelter of dove-wings,
which well may be, since war's meat-grinder
is now the prerogative of small nations,
since, after manifold combinations,
Mars has moved closer to palms and cacti,
and I myself wouldn't hurt a housefly,
not even in summer, its houseflown heyday –
in short, if I do not die from a bullet,
if I die, pajama'd, on my own pillow,
since the land of my birth is a major power –

II

– in some twenty years, when my children no longer
can live on the glow of their father's laurels,
but will earn their own way – I shall be so bold as
to leave my family – in just twenty seasons.
Under watch and ward for my loss of reason,
I shall walk, if my strength holds out, to the building
that has a pharmacy on the corner,
to find the one thing in the whole of Russia
that reminds me of you – even though I'm breaking
the rule: don't go back for what others abandon.

III

In manners and morals this counts as progress.
In some twenty years I shall fetch the armchair[1]
that you sat on, facing me, on Good Friday
when, for Christ's body, the cross's torments
at last were ended; you sat and folded

your arms – on that fifth day of Holy Week – looking
like some new Napoleon exiled on Elba.
Palm fronds glowed golden at every crossing.
You laid down your arms on your grass-green garment,
avoiding the open-armed risk of passion.

IV

A pose such as yours, though not so intended,
is a most fitting symbol of our existence.
This is not, by any means, immobility.
It's an apotheosis of men as objects,
replacing submissiveness with mere quiet.
This is a new kind of Christian teaching:
one has a duty to guard and cherish
those who consider themselves dead objects,
who won't even wake from their deathlike numbness
at the final sounding of Gabriel's trumpet.

V

It's a habit with prophets to be unhealthy.
Most seers are cripples. To put it briefly:
no more than old Calchas am I a seer.
To prophesy is to sniff a flower –
a cactus or violet – through helmet metal.
It's like learning in Braille your alpha-beta.
A hopeless task. To my groping fingers
there are very few objects that feel much like you
in this empty world. A man's own victims
will tell the same tale as his oracle's visions.

VI

You'll forgive me, I'm sure, for this air of jesting.
It seemed the best method to save strong feelings
from a welter of weak ones. The mode of masking,

which comes from the Greeks, is again in fashion.
At the present time it's the strong who perish,
while the tribes of the weak multiply both wholesale
and retail. Take this as my up-to-dating,
my subtle *postscriptum* to Darwin's teaching
(an hypothesis already stiff and cracking);
consider this the new law of the jungle.

VII

In some twenty years, for to call to mind what
is absent is easier than to make it
good by supplying a thing that's novel
– the absence of law is much worse than your absence –
I shall stare my fill like some modern Gogol,
never glancing back, having no misgivings,
as the magic lantern of Christ's own passion,
at the sound of drops from the dripping faucet,
lights up the back of the empty armchair
as though it were meant for a movie screening.

VIII

In our past there is greatness – but prose in our future.
For one asks no more from an empty armchair
than one would from you who once sat upon it
as calm as the waters of Lago di Garda,[2]
crossing your arms, as I've already written.
The total of all of today's embraces
gives far less of love than the outstretched arms of
Christ on the cross. This lame poet's[3] finding
looms before me in Holy Week, sixty-seven,
blocking my leap to the nineteen-nineties.

IX

If that dove lays no egg and thus fails to save me,
so that I'm left alone in this labyrinthine

retreat, without help from my Ariadne
(for death can have variants, and it's valor
in men to foreknow them), alas, my fate is
to be worthy of being denounced and sentenced
to a term in a work-camp, and dysentery –
but if only it isn't a lie they've told me,
and old Lazarus rose from the dead in truth, then
I too shall rise, rushing for that armchair.

X

But rushing is stupid and sinful. *Vale!*
That is, there is no place to rush to. Surely
so sturdy an armchair can't be disabled.
Here in the East we use chairs and tables
for three generations, not counting losses
from fire and from theft. But the worst of all is
the thought that the chair might be dumped together
with others in storage. If this should ever
take place, I would carve on its back a picture
of a delicate dove, with her mate beside her.

XI

Like a bee in its hive, may your whirling armchair
spin through the night orbit of chairs and tables.
A label's not shameful: through it we approach a
quite new astronomy – *sotto voce!* –
confirmed by long practice in jails and armies:
whatever is branded with names or numbers
provides a firm basis for views unswerving,
and this will apply to both dead and living.
I shall not have to search – a homesick Ulysses –
for armchairs like yours, as for cherished faces.

137

XII

I am not a mere antiquarian, really.
Keep in mind, if this discourse seems long, that freely
to speak of an armchair is but a pretext
for penetrating to other topics.
Great faiths leave behind only holy relics.[4]
Judge then of the vast power of love, if objects
touched by you I now hold, while you live, as holy.
Such a high and elaborate style proves only
that the poet belongs to a major power;
it proves nothing at all concerning his lyre.

XIII

The eagle of Russia without its crown is
no more than a crow. And a muttered groan is
all that remains of its once-proud screaming.
This is old age in eagles; the voice of feeling
has turned to an echo or shade of power.
And love songs are pitched but a little lower.
For love, clearly, is an imperial passion,
and you are one whom – to her great good fortune –
Russia must address in imperial accents.

XIV

The armchair is quietly drinking warmness
from the anteroom. Water drips from the faucet,
drop by drop, as it splashes into the washstand.
An alarm clock chirps modestly near the nightlamp.
The flat empty walls share an even lighting
with flowers by the window, whose shadows are trying
to push the room out through the window's structure.
All this taken together is – now – a picture
of the distant and near, of the deep and shallow,
before we existed. – And what will follow.

XV

I wish you goodnight. May I, too, sleep soundly.
Won't you bid a goodnight to my native country
for settling accounts with me – from that distance
where, by the massing of miles, or simple
miracle, you have been changed to only
a postal address.[5] The trees near my window
murmur; roof silhouettes mark day's ending.
In one's motionless body the mind sometimes opens
dampers in the hand, like stovepipe dampers.
I start. Then my pen pursues you.

XVI

My pen cannot reach you. You're cloud-like, fleeting.
The shape of a girl, for each man, is surely
his soul's shape – you, Muse, can confirm this richly –
implying love's source but, alas, love's ruin,
for souls have no bodies. Which means that you are
still farther away. And my pen can't reach you.
So give me your hand as we part. That's better
than nothing. Our parting is solemn, lofty,
since it is forever. The zither's silent.
Forever is not a word, but a number

whose unending zeroes, when grass grows above us,
will stretch out beyond our small time, our epoch.

1967

1. The suggestive similarity of the Russian word *kreslo* ('armchair')
to *krest* ('cross') cannot be conveyed in English.
2. The Lago di Garda, in Northern Italy, is known for violent
storms which spring up suddenly in calm weather. Brodsky's ex-
pression *LaGardy tishe* ('calmer than the Lago di Garda') echoes the
Russian proverb *Tishe vody, nizhe travy* – 'Calmer than water, lower
(i.e., more humble) than grass'.

3. The reference is to the second of the Mary Magdalene poems in Pasternak's *Dr Zhivago* cycle. Pasternak is called a 'lame poet' because he walked with a slight limp, a fact which he attempted to conceal.

4. The Russian term for 'holy relics (of the saints)' is *moshchi*, which is related etymologically to *moshch* ('power').

5. The reference is to Mlle Véronique's address in Paris.

Part 5

From *Gorbunov and Gorchakov*[1]

II

GORBUNOV AND GORCHAKOV

. . .

'Well! I have given you a dressing down!
There's bitterness in Gorchakov's reproach!'
'But why do you regard this as a sin?
Since sin is what is punished while one lives.
And how can I be punished, when the points
of all life's pains are focused in my breast
as in a prism? When the future seems
to loom unhindered?' 'So, we two are now
attending someone's wake?' 'And so my laugh
is taken as an optimistic sign.'

'Last Judgement?' 'That is just a flashing back
in memory. Like something in a film.
And what's Apocalypse to us! No more
than five months in some wilderness. Yes, I
have squandered half my life, and now, and now
I want to dream of mushrooms from here on.
I'll keep in mind where I must needs give way
before the Flaming Angel of the Earth . . .'[2]
'Pain shatters arrogance.' 'No, not a bit.
The tree of arrogance is fed by pain.'

'Does this mean that you do not fear the dark?'
'It has its landmarks.' 'Will you swear it does?'
'My grasp of such landmarks is intimate.
You can just whistle for them, they're so thick.'
'Resourcefulness engenders vanity.'
'Such aphorisms leave me unconvinced.

A man's soul does not feel the lack of space.'
'You think not? What about dead organisms?'
'I think that a man's soul, while it still lives,
takes on the features of mortality.'

...

1965

1. What follows is a thirty-line excerpt from Canto II and the whole of Canto X of Brodsky's long and powerful poem, written between 1965 and December 1968. The entire poem is in the form of a dialogue, chiefly between Gorbunov and Gorchakov. In this selection the first speaker is Gorchakov and the last Gorbunov. (For further discussion of the poem as a whole, see the Introduction, p. 20.)

2. The reference is to the first of the seven angels of the Apocalypse. Cf. Rev. xvi: 2 – 'The first [angel] went, and poured out his vial [of God's wrath] upon the earth. . . .'

From Gorbunov and Gorchakov

A CONVERSATION ON THE PORCH[1]

'A huge city enveloped in dense gloom.'
'Its streets the crisscrossed lines of children's notebooks.'
'It's here that the enormous madhouse looms.'
'A void within the order of the cosmos.'
'Behind its façade lies a cold courtyard
filled up with firewood, blanketed in snowdrifts.'
'But if things are described by means of words,
then is the courtyard not a conversation?'
'Here one sees men, and creatures driven mad
by ghastly lives within the womb and after
the grave.' 'Have we more than a verbal right
to call our fellow-creatures human beings?'
'Note the expression of their eyes. Their arms
and legs. Their heads and their broad shoulders.'
'Once anything has been given a name,
it's shaped into a part of speech directly.'
'Is that true of the body's parts?' 'It is.'
'And what about this place?' 'It's called a madhouse.'
'And what about these days?' 'They are called days.'
'O, everything is turning to a Sodom

of greedy words. Where do they get the right?'
'The names of things are sinister and threatening.'
'One's head is soon stuffed with these hungry words
which turn upon their things and quite devour them!'
'Without a doubt it makes a man's head spin.'
'Such things for Gorbunov – like seas – aren't healthy.'
'It's not the sea racing upon the shore;
it's only words that hard on words are crowding.'

'Words seem almost to image holy things.'[2]
'If objects could be hung up on some cross, then . . .
Names are a shield against things in the world.'
'Against life's meaning too.' 'Yes, in some measure.'
'Are they a shield against Christ's suffering?'
'Against all suffering.' 'God grant you peace, then!'[3]
'For God Himself did shape His mouth to words . . .
And yet He did defend Himself by speaking.'
'And so Christ's life is full of prophecy.'
'A pledge that we shall not drown in that ocean.'
'There is a double meaning in His death.'
'And thus His death's a synonym, or like one.'

'But what about eternity? Does it
stand on the table like a "he-said", wearing
a Tartar robe?'[4] 'It is the only word
that hasn't wholly swallowed up its object.'
'But is it then a shield against mere words?'
'I scarcely think so.' 'He who seeks salvation
beneath the sheltering Cross will find it there.'
'Not wholly.' 'For the synonym is losing
its power to resurrect.' 'That's true.' 'But what
of love? Can it not block the flood of chatter?'
'You must live in seraphic spheres, or else
you can't distinguish between love and lusting.'
'No word is so without distinctive signs.'
'And nothing can be more impenetrable
than veils of words that have devoured their things;
nothing is more tormenting than men's language.'
'But if we view things more objectively
it may be that we'll come to the conclusion
that words are also things. And thus we're saved!'
'But that is the beginning of vast silence.

And silence is the future of all days
that roll toward speech; yes, silence is the presence
of farewells in our greetings as we touch.
Indeed, the future of our words is silence –
those words which have devoured the stuff of things
with hungry vowels, for things abhor sharp corners.
Silence: a wave that cloaks eternity.
Silence: the future fate of all our loving –
a space, not a dead barrier, but space
that robs the false voice in the blood-stream throbbing
of every echoed answer to its love.
And silence is the present fate of those who
have lived before us; it's a matchmaker
that manages to bring all men together
into the speaking presence of today.
Life is but talk hurled in the face of silence.'
'A squabbling of all motions, of all life.'
'Gloom speaks to gloom and marks a hazy ending.'
'And walls are but protests embodied here,
the very incarnation of objections.'

'A huge city enveloped in dense gloom.'
'The speech of chaos, bodied forth concisely.'
'It's here that the enormous madhouse looms,
a void within the order of the cosmos.'
'Curses on these abominable drafts!'
'Your curses do not wound me, though I hear them;
it is not life, but victory of words
that I find here.' 'And predicates from subjects!'
'So a wild bird soars from its nest to search
for food with which to sate its offspring's hunger.'
'A star has climbed above the plain and seeks
with starry words a more lucid companion.'
'The plain itself, as far as eyes can reach,

converses through the night with postal slowness.'
'But how then does it carry on such talk?'
'With high and low points of the land.' 'How, tell me,
can one divide these talkers of the night –
although to do so makes no sense whatever?'
'The high point of the land is Gorbunov;
the place and voice of Gorchakov are lower.'

1968

1. In this section the interlocutors are *not* Gorbunov and Gor-
chakov, but two unidentified people associated with the mental
hospital – presumably either doctors, attendants, or patients.

2. The Russian term is *moshchi*, literally 'holy relics (of the saints)';
it is related etymologically to the word *moshch* ('power').

3. The Russian expression *Bog s vami*, literally, 'God [be] with you',
is also used in the sense of 'Get along with you'.

4. This is an echo of an earlier remark (in Canto V) to the effect that
the 'he-said' (*skazal*) is as confining as a 'Tartar yoke'.

Post Aetatem Nostram[1]

To Andrei Sergeyev

I

'The Empire is a country for dull fools.'
All traffic has been stopped in preparation
for the Emperor's arrival. A dense crowd
washes against the Legionnaires. Singing
and shouting. The curtains of a palanquin
are drawn; love's object shuns all curious glances.

In a deserted coffee shop behind
the palace a vagrant Greek plays dominoes
with an unshaven crippled veteran.
Parings of light tossed from the street crisscross
the tablecloths; faint echoes of festivity
flutter the blinds. The defeated Greek counts up
his drachmas; his victorious opponent
orders a hard-boiled egg and a pinch of salt.

In a high-ceilinged bedchamber an old
state-merchant tells a young hetaera how
he saw the Emperor. Incredulous,
she laughs aloud. Such is the prelude to
their game of love.

II
THE PALACE

A satyr and a nymph, carved out of marble,
gaze silently into the pool's clear depths,
its mirror-surface flecked with rose petals.

The barefoot Governor, with his own fists,
bloodies the soft nose of the local King
because of the three pigeons baked in dough
(when the meat-pie was cut, they had flown out
and then fallen like stones on the great table).
The holiday is ruined, and perhaps
the Governor's career as well.

The King writhes silently on the wet floor,
pinned by the Governor's tough, sinewy knee.
Rose-fragrance fogs the walls. The servants stare,
like statues, straight ahead, betraying not
the least flicker of interest. Polished stones
give back no clear reflection of the deed.

By the unsteady light of the Northern moon
the vagrant Greek, curled up beside the chimney
on the roof above the palace kitchen, strokes
a cat and watches as two slaves bring out
the corpse of the King's cook, wrapped in rough burlap,
and slowly make their way down to the river.

Dry gravel crackles.
                                    On the roof the man
attempts to hold the cat's jaws shut.

III
A barber whose beloved boy has left him
stares at his own reflection in the mirror;
missing the absent boy, he quite forgets
the lathered face of his lone customer.
'I don't suppose he will come back again.'

Meantime, the customer is calmly dozing,
dreaming Greek dreams – of gods, cithara-players,
athletic contests in gymnasiums where
sharp smell of sweat tickles the nostrils.
                         Swooping
down from the ceiling, a huge housefly circles
the room and, landing on the sleeper's cheeks,
sinks into the white lather – like those poor
peltasts (in Xenophon) into the snowdrifts
of Armenia – and slowly crawls,
past ledges and ravines, up toward the summit,
avoids the crater-mouth, and manages
to gain the very tip of the Greek's nose.

The Greek opens his terrible black eye;
the fly, buzzing with horror, zooms away.

IV
After wet holidays the night is dry.
Like a starved horse, the flapping flag at the gate
grinds wind between its jagged teeth. The lab-
yrinthine, empty streets are bathed in moonlight;
the monster must be sleeping soundly.[2]

The farther out one goes from the great palace
the fewer are the statues and bright pools.
Stuccoed façades are rare. And every door
that opens on a balcony is closed.
Here, too, it seems, walls are the lone night-guardians
of men's peace.

The sound of one's own steps is ominous,
yet vulnerable. The stink of fish pervades
the air. The houses now have all been left
behind.

But the moon-rippled road flows on.
A black felucca prowls across it, cat-like,
dissolving in the dark, to let us know
that, really, there's no sense in venturing
beyond this point.

v

In a 'Message to the Rulers' which is posted
on large billboards a well-known local bard,[3]
seething with indignation, boldly calls
for prompt removal of the Emperor's likeness
(in the very next line of his appeal)
from every copper coin.

The crowd is animated. Youths, gray-haired
old men, men in their prime, and literate
hetaeras – all are quite agreed on this:
'Nothing like this was ever seen before.'
They don't, however, make it clear what sort
of thing they have in mind; do they mean courage,
or – perhaps – servility?

No doubt it is the mark of poetry
to draw no sharp frontier between the two.

A sea-horizon, blue beyond belief.
The rustling of the surf. A naked man,
stretched full-length on a dry and burning rock
like some lizard in March, snaps off the shells
of stolen almonds. Farther off two slaves,
chained hard together, clumsily assist
each other as they shed their tattered clothes,
preparing for a dip. They laugh aloud.
The day is hot beyond belief.

The Greek
slips down from the flat rock, his rolling eyes
like two bright silver drachmas, imaging
a new pair of Dioscuri.[4]

VI

The acoustics here are faultless! Not for nothing
did the builder of the stadium feed the lice
of Lemnos[5] during seventeen long years.

The day, too, is delightful. And the crowd,
having poured itself into a stadium-shape,
freezes and holds its breath, as it drinks in
the abuse which the two fighters in the arena
heap on each other to inflame their tempers;
then they draw swords.

The purpose of the contest is not killing,
but death that is both just and logical.
The laws of drama are transferred to sport.
The acoustics are superb.[6] The stands are filled
with men, no women. Sunlight turns to gold
the tousled lions on the royal box.
The stadium has become one giant ear.

'You are a chunk of carrion!' 'So are you!'
'Offal and carrion!' Here the Governor,
whose face is like a festering udder, laughs.

VII
THE TOWER

The midday air is cool.
The iron spire of the city Tower, its tip
lost in the clouds, serves as a lightning-rod,

a lighthouse, and a flagpole for the flag
of state. Inside there is a roomy prison.

As a rough rule, it has been estimated –
in Persian satrapies, under the Pharaohs,
in Islam, in the Christian epoch too –
that six per cent of the whole population
has suffered either life in prison or death.
Because of this, a century ago
the grandsire of the present Emperor
conceived a project of legal reform.
By special fiat he declared an end
to the death penalty, an evil thing;
reduced from six per cent to only two
the number of those doomed to spend their lives
in jail. The law was like a tax; it did
not differentiate the innocent
from those who had in fact committed crimes.
That was the time the city Tower was built.

A blinding flash of chromium-plated steel.
A shepherd, on the Tower's forty-third floor,
his head thrust through a porthole, sends a smile
of welcome to the sheepdog which has come
to visit him.

VIII
The fountain, which depicts a dolphin leaping
in the open sea, is now entirely dry.
That's understandable: a marble fish
has no real need for water, any more
than water has a need for marble fish.

This is a court-of-arbitration verdict,
noted – like all such verdicts – for its dryness.

Arrayed on the wide marble steps that lead
up to the palace's white colonnade,
a group of dark-skinned local chiefs in gaudy,
crumpled robes await their King's approach –

like scattered flowers on a white tablecloth,
flung from a water-filled glass vase.

The King at last appears. The chiefs stand up
and shake their lances. Kisses, hugs, and smiles.
The King's a bit embarrassed. But dark skin
has this distinct advantage: when it's bruised
it does not show its black-and-blueness.

The vagrant Greek summons a boy to him.
'What are they chattering about?' 'Who, them?'
'Uh-huh.' 'They're thanking him.' 'For what?' The boy
raises his lucid eyes: 'For laying down
new laws against the poor.'

IX
THE CAGED BEAST

The heavy bars which block the lion off
from curious men are an iron variant
on jungle thickets.

Green moss. Drops of metallic dew. A lotus
wrapped in thin lianas.

Here nature is mimicked with special love.
the kind which only men can bring to bear,
since only they can see the difference
between losing one's way in matted jungle
and in an empty desert.

A burly Legionnaire in gleaming armor,
who's standing guard by the white-painted door
(a gurgling sound is clearly heard behind it),
stares through a window at the passing women.
It now begins to seem to him somehow –
he has been standing guard for a full hour –
that all the lovely women passing by
have blended into one.

The large gold letter M which decorates
the door seems small compared to that huge M[7]
which, red-faced with its straining, sits behind
the door with head bent down, inspecting each
detail of its reflection in the swiftly-
flowing waters.

Such flowing waters – with their mirrorings –
are no worse, after all, than sculptors who
have flooded the whole Realm with this reflection.
A clear and gurgling stream. An upside-down
Vesuvius[8] hangs vast above it, slow
to start erupting.

It seems that everything is in a bind.
The Empire's like a trireme in a tight
canal too narrow for it. And its rowers
bang down their oars on the dry land; sharp stones
scrape hard against its hull. No, do not say
that we have run aground! We're still afloat
and moving; yes, we're under way. And no
one overtakes us. Yet, alas, how stark

the contrast with our past Imperial speed!
And how can one not sigh for those past times
when things went much more smoothly,
                              much more smoothly?

XI
A lamp goes out; its wick is smoldering
in the dark room. A thin ribbon of smoke
curls toward the ceiling; at first glance, its whiteness,
in that unleavened dark, would harmonize
with any form of light. Even soot.
                              Outside
the window all night long an Asian rainstorm
roars in the unweeded garden. But the mind
stays dry. So dry that, when it is embraced
by the cold, pallid flame of love, it bursts
into a riotous blaze more rapidly
than thinnest paper or driest kindling.

The ceiling does not see this blinding flash.

A man, leaving behind him neither soot
nor ashes, wades into the dripping darkness
and wanders toward the wicker gate. The silver
voice of a chimney swift summons him back.
In heavy rain he obediently returns
to the great kitchen and, unfastening
his belt, pours the remaining drachmas out
on the iron table. Then he leaves for good.
The bird is silent.

XII
Having decided to cross the frontier,
the Greek got a large sack and, in the square

near the main market, filled it up with cats –
twelve cats, all black. With this meowing, scratch-
ing load he came at night to a dense forest
near the border.

The moon was shining as it always shines
in mid-July. Of course the watchdogs poured
their mournful howls into the great ravine.
The cats stopped squabbling in the sack and nearly
fell silent. Then the Greek spoke quietly:
'May my luck hold. Athena, do thou not

abandon me. Walk thou before me.' To
himself he added: 'I shall use six cats
here at this stretch of the frontier – not one
cat more.' The watchdogs won't go down into
the dense pine groves. As for the border guards,
like soldiers everywhere, they're superstitious.

It all worked out superbly. The whole system:
the moon, the dogs, the cats, the superstition,
and the pine groves – functioned without a hitch.
He gained the high divide. But at the moment
when he stood with one foot across the border,
he realized the thing he had forgotten.

Turning around, he caught sight of the sea.

It lay beneath him, far away. Now men,
in contrast to the other animals,
are capable of leaving what they love
(if only to prove that they are not beasts).
His tears, like dog's saliva, gave away
the secret of his animality:

'O, *Thalassa*!'[9]

But in this wicked world
one must not stand, in moonlight, on a high
divide, unless one wants to be a target.
The Greek, heaving the sack onto his back,
began his slow descent into the depths
of the great continent; what rose to meet him

was not the level sea but crests of pine trees.

20 October 1970

1. Translation of the title: 'After our Epoch'. (*Brodsky's note.*)

2. The Emperor is here pictured as a kind of Minotaur. On the Minotaur as a symbol of evil, see Brodsky's poem *To Diomedes on Scyros* (1967).

3. The Russian *kifared*, from the Greek *kitharōdos* (literally, 'cithara-player'), is a rhetorical term for 'poet'. The reference is to a poem by Andrei Voznesensky, the first line of which is: '*Ubiraite Lenina*' ('Remove Lenin'), and the second line: '*s deneg*!' ('from the money', i.e., from certain ruble notes).

4. The Dioscuri – Castor and Pollux – were, in Greek mythology, a symbol of indissoluble friendship. Their image was used on Greek coins. Greeks of the classical period considered it blasphemous to depict rulers on coins; they depicted only gods, symbols of the gods, or mythological personages. (*Brodsky's note.*)

5. Lemnos: an island in the Aegean Sea which served, and still serves, as a place of exile. (*Brodsky's note.*)

6. A reference to the colloquial use in Russian of the expression *prekrasnaya akustika* ('fine acoustics') to show one's appreciation for profane and colorful languge.

7. The Emperor is on the toilet; his legs, viewed from the front, form an *M*.

8. A pun in the original: *Verzuvii* ('Versuvius') rather than *Vezuvii* ('Vesuvius'), suggesting – as Brodsky points out – the Old Slavic word *verzati*, 'to defecate'.

9. *Thalassa*: Greek for 'sea'. (*Brodsky's note.*)

Nature Morte

Verrà la morte e avrà i tuoi occhi.
    Cesare Pavese

I

People and things crowd in.
Eyes can be bruised and hurt
by people as well as things.
Better to live in the dark.

I sit on a wooden bench
watching the passers-by –
sometimes whole families.
I am fed up with the light.

This is a winter month.
First on the calendar.
I shall begin to speak
when I'm fed up with the dark.

II

It's time. I shall now begin.
It makes no difference with what.
Open mouth. It is better to speak,
although I can also be mute.

What then shall I talk about?
Shall I talk about nothingness?
Shall I talk about days, or nights?
Or people? No, only things,

since people will surely die.
All of them. As I shall.

All talk is a barren trade.
A writing on the wind's wall.

III

My blood is very cold –
its cold is more withering
than iced-to-the-bottom streams.
People are not my thing.

I hate the look of them.
Grafted to life's great tree,
each face is firmly stuck
and cannot be torn free.

Something the mind abhors
shows in each face and form.
Something like flattery
of persons quite unknown.

IV

Things are more pleasant. Their
outsides are neither good
nor evil. And their insides
reveal neither good nor bad.

The core of things is dry rot.
Dust. A wood-borer. And
brittle moth-wings. Thin walls.
Uncomfortable to the hand.

Dust. When you switch lights on,
there's nothing but dust to see.
That's true even if the thing
is sealed up hermetically.

V

This ancient cabinet –
outside as well as in –
strangely reminds me of
Paris's Notre Dame.

Everything's dark within
it. Dustmop or bishop's stole
can't touch the dust of things.
Things themselves, as a rule,

don't try to purge or tame
the dust of their own insides.
Dust is the flesh of time.
Time's very flesh and blood.

VI

Lately I often sleep
during the daytime. My
death, it would seem, is now
trying and testing me,

placing a mirror close
to my still-breathing lips,
seeing if I can stand
non-being in daylight.

I do not move. My thighs
are like two icicles.
The blueness of my veins
has a cold-marble look.

VII

Summing their angles up
as a surprise to us,

things drop away from man's
world – a world made with words.

Things do not move, or stand.
That's our delirium.
Each thing's a space, beyond
which there can be no thing.

A thing can be battered, burned,
gutted, and broken up.
Thrown out. And yet the thing
never will yell, 'O, fuck!'

VIII
A tree. Its shadow, and
earth, pierced by clinging roots.
Interlaced monograms.
Clay and a clutch of rocks.

Roots interweave and blend.
Stones have their private mass
which frees them from the bond
of normal rootedness.

This stone is fixed. One can't
move it, or heave it out.
Tree-shadows catch a man,
like a fish, in their net.

IX
A thing. Its brown color. Its
blurry outline. Twilight.
Now there is nothing left.
Only a *nature morte*.

Death will come and will find
a body whose silent peace
will reflect death's approach
like any woman's face.

Scythe, skull, and skeleton –
an absurd pack of lies.
Rather: 'Death, when it comes
will have your own two eyes.'

x

Mary now speaks to Christ:
'Are you my son? – or God?
You are nailed to the cross.
Where lies my homeward road?

How can I close my eyes,
uncertain and afraid?
Are you dead? – or alive?
Are you my son? – or God?'

Christ speaks to her in turn:
'Whether dead or alive,
woman, it's all the same –
son or God, I am thine.'

1971

Nunc Dimittis[1]

When Mary first came to present the Christ Child
to God in His temple, she found – of those few
who fasted and prayed there, departing not from it –
    devout Simeon and the prophetess Anna.

The holy man took the Babe up in his arms.
The three of them, lost in the grayness of dawn,
now stood like a small shifting frame that surrounded
    and guarded the Child in the dark of the temple.

The temple enclosed them in forests of stone.
Its lofty vaults stooped as though trying to cloak
the prophetess Anna, and Simeon, and Mary –
    to hide them from men and to hide them from Heaven.

A chance ray of light struck the crown of the head
of that sleeping Infant, who stirred but as yet
was conscious of nothing. He blew drowsy bubbles;
    old Simeon's arms held him like a stout cradle.

It had been revealed to this upright old man
that he would not die until his eyes had seen
the Son of the Lord. And it thus came to pass. And
    he said: 'Now, o Lord, lettest thou thy poor servant,

according to thy holy word, leave in peace,
for mine eyes have witnessed thine offspring, this Child –
in him thy salvation, which thou hast made ready,
    a light to enlighten the face of all peoples

and carry thy truth to idolatrous tribes;
bring Israel, thy people, its Glory in time.'
Then Simeon paused. A thick silence engulfed them,
    and only his echoing words grazed the rafters,

to spin for a moment, with faint rustling sounds,
high over their heads in the tall temple's vaults,
like some soaring bird that flies constantly upward
    and somehow is caught and cannot return earthward.

A strangeness engulfed them. The silence now seemed
as strange and uncanny as Simeon's speech.
And Mary, confused and bewildered, said nothing –
    so strange had his words been. The holy man, turning

to Mary, continued: 'Behold, in this Child,
now close to thy breast, is concealed the great fall
and rising again of the many in Israel;
    a source of dissension, a sign to be spoken

against. The same weapon which tears at his flesh
shall pierce through thine own soul as well.
Thy wound, Mary, like a new eye, will reveal to
    thy sight what in men's deepest hearts now lies hidden.'

He ended and moved toward the temple's great door.
Old Anna, bent down with the weight of her years,
and Mary, gazed after him, perfect in silence.
    He moved and grew smaller, in size and in meaning,

to these two frail women who stood in the gloom.
As though driven on by the force of their looks,
he strode through the cold empty space of the temple
    and moved toward the whitening blur of the doorway.

The stride of his old legs was audibly firm.
He slowed his step slightly when Anna began
to speak, far behind him. But she was not calling
   to him; she had started to bless God and praise Him.

The door came still closer. The wind stirred his robe
and touched his cool brow, while the roar of the street,
exploding in life by the door of the temple,
   beat stubbornly into old Simeon's hearing.

He went forth to die. It was not the loud din
of streets that he faced when he flung the door wide,
but rather the deaf-and-dumb fields of death's kingdom.
   He strode through a space that was no longer solid.

The roaring of time ebbed away in his ears.
And Simeon's soul held the form of the Child –
its feathery crown now enveloped in glory –
   aloft, like a torch, pressing back the black shadows,

to light up the path that leads into death's realm,
where never before until this point in time
had any man managed to lighten his pathway.
   The old man's torch glowed and the pathway grew wider.

16 February 1972[2]

   1. This poem – titled in the original *Sreten'e* ('The Presentation [in the Temple]') – is based on the account in Luke ii: 22–36, which Brodsky considers the point of transition from the Old Testament to the New. Simeon's speech in the fifth and sixth stanzas is the *Nunc dimittis* ('Now lettest thou thy servant depart . . .') found in most Christian liturgies.
   2. The date February 16 (on the New Calendar; or February 3, on the Old) is the Feast Day of Saints Simeon and Anna, and hence the Name Day of Anna Akhmatova – a point which Brodsky wishes to emphasize.

Odysseus to Telemachus

My dear Telemachus,
                 The Trojan War
is over now; I don't recall who won it.
The Greeks, no doubt, for only they would leave
so many dead so far from their own homeland.
But still, my homeward way has proved too long.
While we were killing time there, old Poseidon,
it almost seems, stretched and extended space.

I don't know where I am or what this place
can be. It would appear some filthy island,
with bushes, buildings, and great grunting pigs.
A garden choked with weeds; some queen or other.
Grass and huge stones . . . Telemachus, dear boy!
To a wanderer the faces of all islands
resemble one another. The mind trips
when it counts waves; eyes, stung by sea horizons,
must weep; and flesh of water stuffs one's ears.
I can't remember how the war came out;
even how old you are—I can't remember.

Grow up, then, my Telemachus, grow strong.
Only the gods know if we'll see each other
again. You've long since ceased to be that babe
before whom I reined in the pawing bullocks.
Had it not been for Palamedes' trick
we two would still be living in one household.
But maybe he was right; away from me
you are quite safe from all Oedipal passions,
and your dreams, my Telemachus, are blameless.

1972

168

Index of Titles

Index of First Lines

73 74 75 76 77 10 9 8 7 6 5 4 3 2 1